COLLINS GEM GUIDES

General Editor
Jeff Daniels

COLLINS
London and Glasgow

First published 1986
Wm Collins Sons and Co Ltd

© Chevprime Ltd

Produced by Chevprime Ltd
147 Cleveland Street
London W1

ISBN 0 00 458835 5

Printed by New Interlitho, Italy

Contents

Introduction

People have always argued over the definition of a sports car. For the purpose of this selection we have taken as a guideline the idea that a sports car is one which sacrifices comfort, convenience and (quite often) ease of driving in order to be able to go faster and handle better than ordinary saloon cars of similar price.

The most obvious sacrifice of convenience is to have only two seats instead of four. By having to find less space for seats, you should be able to make your

car smaller and lighter, and thus gain in performance. It also used to be the case that you could save weight by cutting off the car's roof and fitting a light canvas hood; hence the still-popular picture of the sports car as an open-topped two-seater of the kind typified by the 1930s MG. Yet the switch in car design away from the separate chassis and into more efficient 'unitary' construction meant that such a convertible car might well be heavier than an equivalent with a closed steel roof which could play its own part in making the vehicle stronger and stiffer.

MG Midget

The new generation of small convertible saloons which emerged in the early 1980s was aimed simply at people who enjoyed open-air motoring, and made no pretence of being 'sporting' according to our definition.

The sports car has diversified in other ways which take it outside the spirit of our definition. The highest-performance sports cars have always been expensive, but in the 1950s there emerged a new breed of 'Grand Touring' (GT) car whose aim was to combine sporting performance with great comfort and luxury. Such cars pose a special problem for anyone tracing the history of the sports car. It is

tempting to say that anything above a certain price should be excluded, but you quickly find that excludes some of the finest sporting (and therefore, arguably, sports) cars built since the end of the last war. What we have done with the GT brigade, therefore, is to include those cars which were two-seaters whose main appeal was ultra-high performance. Even then, since all the best rules are made to be broken, we have included the Aston Martin Vantage which, despite being a four-seater, comes closest of all current cars to the traditional idea of a sports car for real he-men – rich ones, of course.

If anything, we have drawn a firmer line before the

Aston Martin Vantage

specialised sports-racing car. At one time, sports-car racing was just that: events for open two-seaters which were – or at least, could have been – driven to the track on public roads. However, the changes in sporting regulations as they tried to keep track of ever more ingenious 'rule-bending' by those who most wanted to win, resulted by the 1960s in a generation of 'sports' cars which were barely, if at all, able to be driven legally on ordinary public roads. The products of such firms such as Chevron and Lola fall entirely into this category, as do the equivalent models from (for instance) Ferrari and Porsche, and others like the Ford GT40. All these specialised track-racers have been excluded.

So how did the sports car really begin? You could argue that in the pioneer days of motoring, everything was a sports car. Most of the car bodies built before World War I were open-topped, and motoring was still expensive enough to be regarded as a rich man's hobby. Such races as were run for road-going cars were mostly entered by versions with the bodywork stripped down to a bare minimum: look, for instance, at the 60hp Mercedes which is widely regarded as 'the first true sports car' with reason. Meanwhile, in America, the advent of the Ford Model T had meant that motoring was no longer the preserve of the rich enthusiast. That meant that some car manufacturers were keen to offer models which went fast, and handled better, than the 'Tin Lizzie' which, to be fair, was not a difficult thing to achieve). Thus, whatever we Europeans like to think, some of the earliest real sports cars to be built in any quantity appeared in the USA: the Mercer Raceabout and the Stutz Bearcat, for instance.

It was only after the end of World War I that the golden age of the sports car dawned in Europe. As cars became more common, so more drivers wanted something that would enable them to indulge their enthusiasm. The standard small saloon cars of those days were very crude devices and it was not difficult for a skilled engineer to effect improvements to both chassis and engine. It is worth remembering that Jaguar began by converting Austin Sevens into something more sporting and that the first MGs were nothing more than converted, rebodied Morris saloons.

At the same time, more expensive tastes were being catered for by a wide variety of cars designed by engineers who realised they could do better still by starting with a 'clean sheet of paper'. The 1920s were also the days in which a small-scale production line could be started up without incurring the huge costs which later made it almost impossible for a newcomer to break into car manufacturing. Thus the 1920s saw the rise of companies like AC, Aston Martin, Frazer-Nash and Lea-Francis in Britain. Amilcar, Delage, Hotchkiss and Salmson in France and Alfa Romeo in Italy. They were also the greatest of days for the engineering genius of Bugatti, who achieved sporting performance through light weight,

attention to detail and an uncanny feeling for chassis design at a time when very little was known about why cars handled as they did. At the other end of the scale was Bentley, whose cars Bugatti called 'the fastest lorries in the world' – partly in pique no doubt at Bentley's long string of successes at Le Mans.

As the 1930s wore on, the 'cheap' sports cars became better and the choice wider. The MG was joined by equivalent models from Riley and Singer.

Mercedez-Benz SSK Roadster

Nor should we overlook the Morgan, which established the shape which still sells today. It was also an age of large and splendid cars like the French Delahaye, which challenged the Bentley tradition, while America threw up its own crop of sporting cars which have since become sought-after and valued

11

classics: Auburn, Cord and Duesenberg. Germany staked its own claim with a succession of formidable models from Mercedes, plus lighter and more nimble designs from companies like BMW.

With the conclusion of World War II, a great deal had changed. The French motor industry was too concerned with basic recovery to be interested in sports cars, the Germans even more so. The classic American names had vanished or been absorbed into the 'big four' manufacturers. Through the 1950s it was largely the British and the Italians who kept the sports car tradition alive. The British probably most of all with a succession of deftly-timed strokes (even if most of them actually came about by happy accident) which injected new life into the formula each time it looked as though it might be dying. We saw the Jaguar XK120, the Healey 100, the Triumph TR2 and finally the Austin-Healey Sprite, which one after the other offered the motorist the chance of real excitement at affordable prices. In Italy, the same period saw the emergence of Ferrari as a force in sports car development, along with his great rivals at Maserati.

The 1960s were another era of change. Some of the last of the traditional sports car names, like MG, were almost allowed to die by their mass-production masters, or ended up as mere higher-performance versions of standard saloons. Yet at the same time there were new developments from engineers like Colin Chapman, surely the nearest post-war equivalent to Bugatti in the way he advanced the understanding of chassis and suspension design. Chapman's Lotus Cars gained real stature with the Elite and Elan, and moved on to more modern cars in the GT mould. It was also a decade of expansion for the Italian GT industry, with names like de Tomaso, Lamborghini and Iso joining the longer-established companies; while in Germany it became obvious that Porsche was a force to be reckoned with, as the 911 made a name for itself.

In America the situation was different. There was no question of a small-volume specialist gaining even a toehold in that massive market, yet there was a huge potential demand for a value-for-money sporting car (as opposed to General Motors' highly specialised Corvette). Eventually Ford tapped that market with a brilliant piece of improvisation called the Mustang, which created new sales records as soon as it was introduced. In the worthy tradition of so many 1920s sports cars, the Mustang owed most of its mechanical components to ordinary production saloon cars, yet it offered that most important of sporting ingredients, sheer fun in driving. It was also steadily developed to achieve formidable performance. General Motors could hardly allow itself to be outclassed, and quickly had the rival Chevrolet Camaro and Pontiac Firebird on sale. Were any of them really sports cars? By our definition, and in the eyes of most American buyers, certainly.

Yet for all the success of what became known as

the 'muscle cars' it seemed to one major manufacturer that there was also a very large demand for a two-seater coupé in a more classic mould. That manufacturer was Japan's Datsun, and it did what nobody else had dared to do — spend money equipping for the large-scale production of a two-seater using the most modern techniques. The result was the 240Z which became such an outstanding success.

Meanwhile, European designers in particular were beginning to think the only way to build a sports car which would handle better than the best modern saloons would be to change the layout of the vehicle fundamentally and put the engine amidships, aft of the cabin but forward of the (driven) rear wheels. Some of the cars which used this formula — Ferrari Dino, Fiat X1/9, Lancia Stratos, Maserati Merak — certainly seemed to promise an extension of the sports car concept towards the year 2000; yet some of their rivals, like Porsche, Datsun and Alfa Romeo steered clear of the mid-engined layout. It is a question which remains to be resolved, but then the sports car is always throwing up that kind of question. Almost certainly the next will be this: can a car with four-wheel drive be considered a true sports car? There can be no final answer to that sort of question. The best thing you can do is to look through this book, gain for yourself some idea of the shape of the sports car tradition and come up with your own conclusions.

List of abbreviations

bhp	brake horse power
cc	cubic capacity
cm	centimetres
GP	Grand Prix
ifs	independent front suspension
ioe	inlet overhead exhaust
km/h	kilometres per hour
mph	miles per hour
mm	millimetres
ohc	overhead camshaft
ohv	overhead valves
rpm	revs per minute

MERCER Type 35 Raceabout

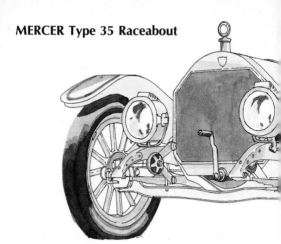

Country of Origin: USA
Date: 1911
Engine: Straight four; side valves in T head; one carburettor; 58bhp at 1,700rpm; dual ignition
Gears: three-speed manual
Capacity: 4,916cc
Bore & Stroke: 111 × 127mm
Maximum Speed: 113km/h (70mph)
Chassis: pressed steel side members. Front and rear suspension comprising semi-elliptic springs and friction dampers

Dimensions: wheelbase 274cm (108in). Track 145cm (57in)
Brakes: rear wheel drum; transmission brake

The Raceabout was the most prestigious model of the Mercer Type 35 series, designed by Finlay Robertson Porter. Its long flowing lines gave the Raceabout the spirited look which was typical of the sports cars of a later era. It sold very well and later became one of the most sought-after pre-World War I models. Racing versions were also made, and in 1914 Eddie Pullen won the American Grand Prix in a Type 35.

VAUXHALL Prince Henry E-type 30/98

Country of Origin: Great Britain
Date: 1913
Engine: straight four, 4.5-litre; side valves; one carburettor; 90bhp at 3,000rpm
Gears: separate four-speed manual
Capacity: 4,525cc
Bore & Stroke: 98 × 150mm
Maximum Speed: 130km/h (80mph)
Chassis: pressed steel side members. Front and rear suspension comprising semi-elliptic leaf springs and friction dampers
Dimensions: wheelbase 295cm (116in). Track 137cm (54in)

Brakes: rear wheel drum; transmission brake
This car scored many early sprint and hillclimb successes, driven by John Higginson, a textile engineer from Stockport. After World War I the 30/98 was England's premier sporting car, developing away from the spartan pre-war model and eventually acquired the famous Velox four-seater body with its Extraordinary grace and subtlety. The car was high-geared, and cruising at 104km (65mph) was both quiet and comfortable.

STUTZ Bearcat Speedster

Country of Origin: USA
Date: 1914
Engine: straight four; side valves in T head; 60bhp at 1,500rpm
Gears: three-speed manual
Capacity: 6,396cc
Bore & Stroke: 121 × 140mm
Maximum Speed: 137km/h (85mph)
Chassis: pressed steel side members. Front and rear suspension by semi-elliptic springs
Dimensions: wheelbase 333cm (131in). Track (front) 144cm (56.5in); track (rear) 149cm (58.5in)

The Stutz Bearcat was one of the most famous cars of the vintage period. The only other cars which could rival its speed and style were the Mercers, and in fact the Bearcat took over a good deal of the Mercer Raceabout market. In 1915 some Bearcats in motorsport form were fitted with overhead camshafts and four valves per cylinder. They had a vigorous and successful racing career up until 1919, when Harry Stutz sold the company to a financial consortium.

SILVER HAWK

Country of Origin: Great Britain
Date: 1920
Engine: Coventry-Simplex, four-cylinder, 1½-litre; side valves; 10.8hp
Gears: three-speed
Capacity: 1,498cc
Bore & Stroke: 66 × 109.5mm
Maximum Speed: 113km/h (70mph)
Chassis: channel-section steel. Front and rear suspension semi-elliptic leaf springs
Dimensions: wheelbase 244cm (96in)
Tyres: 71 × 9cm

Steering: worm-and-sector
Brakes: rear wheel drum; transmission brake
Body: two-seater

Although the Silver Hawk was a short-lived project and very few were built, it made its mark on the British sports-car scene while it lasted. It had an attractive, two-seater body with an outside exhaust pipe, extended front wings and a pointed tail. It was raced at Brooklands and at Le Mans with some success. It had a reputation for speed and reliability, but despite this, the company went out of business in 1921.

BUGATTI 'Brescia' Type 22

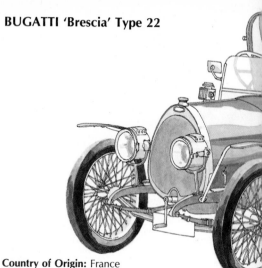

Country of Origin: France
Date: 1922
Engine: four-cylinder; ohc; 40bhp at 3,800rpm
Gears: four-speed
Capacity: 1,453cc
Bore & Stroke: 68 × 100mm
Maximum Speed: 145km/h (90mph)
Dimensions: wheelbase 196cm (77in)
Although by 1926 it was just about obsolete, during
its short career as a production car the Brescia Type

22 was one of the fastest small cars on the market. It had had a lengthy history before its reputation as a production car became established. It had been tested experimentally in a slightly modified form as early as 1914, and was enormously successful in the International 'Grand Prix des Voiturettes' at Brescia in Italy in 1921. It was this success which gave it its name.

DELAGE DISS

Country of Origin: France
Date: 1922
Engine: straight four; pushrod; single carburettor; 48bhp at 3,200rpm.
Gears: four-speed manual
Capacity: 2,121cc
Bore & Stroke: 75 × 120mm
Chassis: pressed steel side members with cruciform bracing. Front and rear suspension by semi-elliptic springs and dampers

Dimensions: wheelbase 299cm (118in). Track 131cm (51.5in)
Brakes: four-wheel drum
The DISS (Sport Surbaissé) had several notable features including a Ducellier dynamotor (starter-generator), an elegant nickel-silver radiator and Rudge wire wheels. Steering was light and it had good roadholding capacity. It was a heavy vehicle which impaired acceleration, but despite this a high cruising speed was obtainable.

ASTON MARTIN 1923

Country of Origin: Great Britain
Date: 1923
Engine: Coventry-Simplex four-cylinder, 1.5-litre; side valves; 35bhp at 4,000rpm; SU carburettor
Gears: four-speed manual
Capacity: 1,486cc
Bore & Stroke: 66.5 × 107mm
Maximum Speed: 113km/h (70mph)
Chassis: Isotta-Fraschini voiturette. Front and rear suspension comprising semi-elliptic springs
Dimensions: wheelbase 267cm (105in). Track 129.54cm (51in)

Originally designed in 1922 for Count Zborowski, who controlled the company's finances, this car failed to make any impression in races in that year, and in 1923 was made available to other private customers. By 1926 the company which built it, Bamford and Martin, had been bought by W.S. Renwick (an engineer) who, along with fellow engineer Bertelli, produced a range of 1½-litre Aston Martins up until the mid-1930s, establishing a good competition record at Brooklands, Le Mans and the Mille Miglia.

BALLOT 2LS

Country of Origin: France
Date: 1924
Engine: four cylinders, in line; 2-litre; four ohvs per cylinder; twin ohcs; 75bhp at 4,000rpm.
Gears: four-speed manual
Capacity: 1,995cc
Bore & Stroke: 70 × 130mm
Maximum Speed: 148km/h (92mph)
Chassis: pressed steel side members. Front and rear suspension comprising semi-elliptic springs

The Ballot brothers, Edouard and Maurice, began by manufacturing marine engines. They became involved in motor racing after World War I. With ex-Peugeot engineer Henry, they built a straight eight 4.9-litre car for the French Grand Prix in 1921. Later they developed a 2-litre racing car, and a touring version was evolved from this, the 2LS.

BENTLEY 'Red Label' Speed Model

Country of Origin: Great Britain
Date: 1925
Engine: straight four, 3-litre; single ohc; single or twin SU carburettors; 85bhp at 3,500rpm
Gears: separate four-speed manual
Capacity: 2,996cc
Bore & Stroke: 80 × 149mm
Maximum Speed: 160km/h (100mph)
Chassis: pressed steel side members. Front and rear suspension by semi-elliptic springs with friction dampers

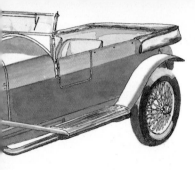

Dimensions: wheelbase 298cm (117.5in). Track 142cm (56in)
Brakes: four-wheel drum
Body: Vanden Plas four-seat sports bodywork
The 'Red Label' was the radiator badge which signified the Speed Model short-chassis Bentley. W.O. Bentley had closely studied the 1914 Grand Prix-winning Mercedes engine, which was in many ways ahead of its time, and made improvements in it to produce an engine capable of sustained performance on both road and track.

DIATTO Tipo 20

Country of Origin: Italy
Date: 1925
Engine: straight four, 2-litre; ohv with single ohc; 45bhp at 2,700rpm
Gears: four-speed
Capacity: 1,996cc
Bore & Stroke: 80 × 100mm
Maximum Speed: 100km/h (62mph)

Chassis: front suspension, semi-elliptic springs. Rear suspension cantilever springs
Dimensions: wheelbase 269cm (106in)
Brakes: front wheel brakes
Throughout the 1920s Dialto produced a series of superb cars partly designed by Alfieri Maserati, who established his own company in 1926. There was also a 2,980cc four-cylinder model, of which only a few were built.

OM T665 Superba

Country of Origin: Italy
Date: 1925
Engine: straight six, 2-litre; side valves; one Zenith carburettor; 45bhp at 3,500rpm
Gears: four-speed manual
Capacity: 1,991cc
Bore & Stroke: 65 × 100mm
Chassis: pressed steel side members. Front and rear suspension comprising semi-elliptic springs and friction dampers

Dimensions: wheelbase 310cm (122in). Track 132cm (52in)
Brakes: four-wheel drum

The OM 665 Superba had side valves at a time when ohvs were considered to be essential in a respectable sports car. It proved its mettle when six-cylinder OMs came fourth and fifth at Le Mans in 1926, first, second and third in the first Mille Miglia Race in 1927, and second in the 1928 Mille Miglia. However, by 1928, despite improvements, the OMs were no match for the Alfas and Bugattis.

BENTLEY Super Sports

Country of Origin: Great Britain
Date: 1926
Engine: four-cylinders, in line; 3-litre; ohv; ohc; two SU carburettors; 80bhp at 3,500rpm
Gears: four-speed, manual
Capacity: 2,996cc
Bore & Stroke: 80 × 149mm
Maximum Speed: 160km/h (100mph)
Chassis: front and rear suspension semi-elliptic springs

Dimensions: wheelbase 274cm (108in). Track 142cm (56in)
Tyres: 13.3 × 53cm
Brakes: four-wheel drum
The Bentley Super Sports was a variant of the legendary Bentley 3-litre. It had a shorter chassis than the Speed Model of the previous year and a distinctive tapering radiator; however, its handling was uncertain. Only a few were built.

SALMSON Grand Sport

Country of Origin: France
Date: 1926
Engine: straight four; ohv; two ohcs
Gears: three-speed manual
Capacity: 1,086cc
Bore & Stroke: 62 × 90mm
Maximum Speed: 113km/h (70mph)
Chassis: front suspension, semi-elliptic springs. Rear suspension, quarter-elliptic springs
Dimensions: wheelbase 254cm (100in). Track 114cm (45in)
Brakes: four-wheel

Salmsons of all types were very popular, cheap vehicles throughout the 1920s. Along with the Grand Sport Special (1926) and the Grand Prix, the Grand Sport was one of the truely sporty versions of the Salmson range. With a reputation for reliability, it could exceed 113km/h (70mph) and was successful in many different types of motor sport including trials, rallies, sprints and track racing.

SUNBEAM 3-litre Super Sports

Country of Origin: Great Britain
Date: 1926
Engine: six cylinders, in line; 3-litre; ohv; two ohcs; two carburettors; 90bhp at 3,800rpm
Gears: four-speed, manual
Capacity: 2,916cc
Bore & Stroke: 75 × 110mm
Maximum Speed: 136km/h (85mph)
Chassis: front suspension semi-elliptic springs. Rear suspension comprising cantilever springs

The engine of this famous and handsome model was derived from the successful Grand Prix engine designed by Bertarione. It was entered in the 1925 Le Mans 24-Hour Race where it came second, beating even the 3-litre Bentley in the process. It went into production late in 1925 as possibly the first production model with two overhead camshafts available generally. Its two main problems were its weak chassis and its cantilever rear springs which did not improve roadholding.

BUGATTI Type 37

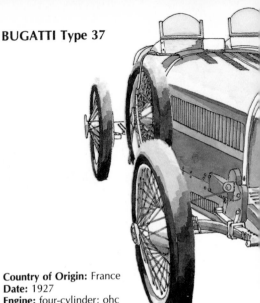

Country of Origin: France
Date: 1927
Engine: four-cylinder; ohc
Gears: four-speed
Capacity: 1,496cc
Bore & Stroke: 60 × 100mm
Chassis: front suspension by semi-elliptic springs.
Rear suspension by reversed quarter-elliptic springs
Dimensions: wheelbase 240cm (94.5in)
Tyres: 11 × 68.6cm

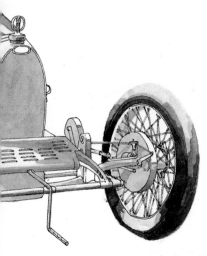

From the Bugatti vintage era the Type 37, along with the 35, 39, 43 and 49, was an outstanding sports car. Like all Bugattis, it possessed superlative roadholding abilities achieved without independent front suspension. The chassis exhibited the legendary Bugatti artistry and finesse, with an economy and fitness of purpose second to none for its time.

RILEY Nine Brooklands

Country of Origin: Great Britain
Date: 1927
Engine: straight four; pushrod ohv; twin Solex carburettors; 50bhp at 5,000rpm
Gears: four-speed manual
Capacity: 1,089cc
Bore & Stroke: 6.3 × 95.2mm
Maximum Speed: 130km/h (80mph)
Chassis: pressed steel side members, underslung at rear. Front and rear suspension comprising of semi-elliptic leaf springs, friction dampers
Dimensions: wheelbase 244cm (96in). Track 121cm (47.5in)

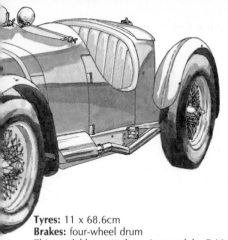

Tyres: 11 x 68.6cm
Brakes: four-wheel drum

This model became the epitome of the British sports car. It had a low-slung, rakish appearance with flared front wings. The first few cars were actually assembled at Brooklands by the firm of Thomson & Taylor, but later on, Riley took over production themselves. The engine, which caused a sensation when it appeared, remained the basis of Riley models until 1957. Development work was undertaken by Parry Thomas, the famous Welsh driver-engineer. He was killed in 1927 while attempting the Land Speed Record, and subsequently Reid Railton took over.

47

AMILCAR CGSs

Country of Origin: France
Date: 1928
Engine: four vertical cylinders, in line; side valves;
35bhp at 4,500rpm
Gears: three- or four-speed
Capacity: 1,074cc
Bore & Stroke: 60 × 95mm
Maximum Speed: 129km/h (80mph)
Chassis: front suspension by semi-elliptic springs.
Rear suspension by quarter-elliptic springs
Brakes: four-wheel

This car evolved from the famous CGS Grand Sport of 1924. The last 's' stood for *surbaissé*, because it had a lowered chassis and radiator. It was in production from 1926 to 1929, being dropped by the company because fashions changed and its spartan sporting style was no longer popular. A few cars were built supercharged at 40bhp, with pump cooling. The 1927 Monte Carlo Rally was won by a blown cabriolet version.

MG M-type Midget

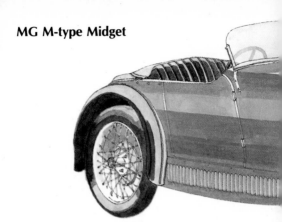

Country of Origin: Great Britain
Date: 1928
Engine: straight four; single ohc; one SU carburettor;
20bhp at 4,000rpm
Gears: three-speed manual
Capacity: 847cc
Bore & Stroke: 57 × 83mm
Maximum Speed: 105km/h (65mph)
Chassis: pressed steel side members. Front and rear
suspension by semi-elliptic springs and friction
dampers
Dimensions: wheelbase 198cm (78in). Track 107cm
(42in)

Brakes: four-wheel drum

The M-type was the first MG Midget and was closely based on the Morris Minor. It had a boat-tailed style, influenced by contemporary GP racing cars, and fixed cycle wings, vee screen and a fabric-covered body. It used the Minor chassis and suspension, and its modest price and good speeds ensured that it was a bestseller.

MORGAN Super Sports

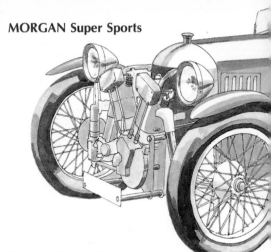

Country of Origin: Great Britain
Date: 1928
Engine: JAP, V-2; pushrod ohv; 50bhp at 4,000rpm
Gears: three-speed manual
Capacity: 1,096cc
Bore & Stroke: 85.7 × 95mm
Maximum Speed: 129km/h (80mph)
Chassis: tubular. Independent front suspension comprising coil springs as sliding axles. Rear suspension quarter-elliptic leaf springs
Dimensions: wheelbase 183cm (72in)

Tyres: 10 × 68.5cm
Brakes: three-wheel brakes

The Morgan concern turned out its beautiful and popular little three-wheelers for longer than any other firm in the three-wheeler market, they were still in production in 1936. The 1928 JAP-engined model was the hottest of its kind. Its chassis was longer and lower than the other Morgans and it had a wider track. The fastest speeds in this car were achieved by Mrs Gwenda Stewart who, in addition to breaking many records at Montlhéry, became the fastest Morgan driver of either sex by doing a mean kilometre speed of 115.6 (72mph) in 1930.

ALFA ROMEO 6C Super Sport

Country of Origin: Italy
Date: 1929
Engine: straight six; 85bhp at 4,500rpm; Roots-type supercharger; twin ohcs
Gears: four-speed manual
Capacity: 1,750cc
Bore & Stroke: 65 × 88mm
Maximum Speed: 145km/h (90mph)
Chassis: pressed steel side members; semi-elliptic springs and friction dampers front and rear

Dimensions: wheelbase 274cm (108in). Track 137cm (54in)
Tyres: 71 × 14cm
Brakes: four-wheel drum
This model had a string of racing successes from the start. It won the Mille Miglia in 1929 and 1930, and was second in 1931. It also won the Spa 24-Hour Race in 1929 and 1930, and was second in 1931. Other successes were the Irish Grand Prix in 1929, the Ulster Tourist Trophy Race in 1930; it gained second place in the Targa Florio in 1931.

CORD L29

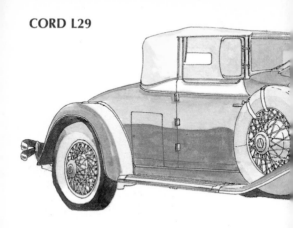

Country of Origin: USA
Date: 1929
Engine: Lycoming, eight vertical cylinders, in line; side valves; front wheel drive
Gears: three-speed
Capacity: 4,800cc
Bore & Stroke: 82,5 × 114mm
Chassis: front suspension by four quarter-elliptic springs. Rear suspension by semi-elliptic springs
Dimensions: wheelbase 348cm (137in)
Brakes: Lockheed hydraulic

The L29 was designed to fill a sales gap between the Auburn and Duesenberg cars. There were four standard models — brougham, cabriolet, phaeton and sedan, there were also some boat-tailed speedsters. Unfortunately for this sleek and powerful car, it was introduced at a bad time for the market, coming as it did at the time of the Stock Market crash. The L29 was phased out three years later, 4,429 having been built.

DUPONT Model G

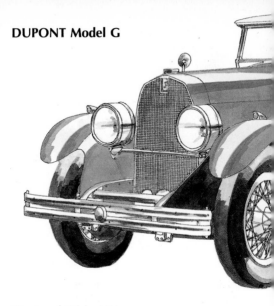

Country of Origin: USA
Date: 1929
Engine: Continental straight eight, 5.2-litre; 140bhp at 3,600rpm; side valves
Gears: three- or four-speed
Capacity: 5,274cc
Bore & Stroke: 85.7 × 114.3mm

Maximum Speed: 183km/h (114mph)
Dimensions: wheelbase 279cm (110in)
Body: two-seater 'speedster'. Many other body styles available. Horizontally barred radiator grille

This was DuPont's best-known model, although the company produced only 537 of its luxury cars in total. Apart from the Model G, it produced a 4.1-litre side valve, four-cylinder model and proprietary six-cylinder models.

LEA-FRANCIS Hyper Sports (S-type)

Country of Origin: Great Britain
Date: 1929
Engine: Meadows four-cylinder, in line; Cozette supercharger; pushrod operated ohvs; 61bhp at 4,100rpm
Gears: four-speed
Capacity: 1,496cc
Bore & Stroke: 69 × 100mm
Maximum Speed: 153km/h (95mph)

Chassis: front and rear suspension by semi-elliptic springs
Body: two-seater, fabric-covered ash frame
This was the model which established the company's ability to produce powerful cars and was beloved of enthusiasts in its day. Kaye Don won his famous victory in the 1928 Tourist Trophy Race in a beefed-up version. The Hyper Sports represented the vintage car at its best.

MERCEDES-BENZ SSK

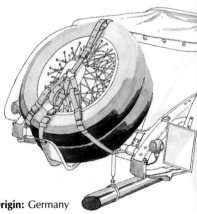

Country of Origin: Germany
Date: 1929
Engine: straight six; single ohc; twin carburettors and Roots-type supercharger; 225bhp at 3,300rpm
Gears: four-speed manual
Capacity: 7,069cc
Bore & Stroke: 100 x 150mm
Maximum Speed: 200km/h (125mph)
Chassis: pressed steel side members. Front and rear suspension comprising semi-elliptic springs; hydraulic friction dampers

Dimensions: wheelbase 295cm (116in). Track 141cm (55.5in)

Brakes: four-wheel drum, with servo assistance

The SSK was a development of the massive 1928 SS model which could achieve 177km/h (110mph). The SSK was developed as a lightweight short-chassis competition variant. It had a two-seater body and an even larger-capacity supercharger. Caracciola won the 1929 Tourist Trophy at Ards in one of these cars.

MG 18/80 Mk II

Country of Origin: Great Britain
Date: 1929
Engine: straight six; single ohc; twin SU carburettors; 58bhp at 3,200rpm
Gears: four-speed manual
Capacity: 2,468cc
Bore & Stroke: 69 × 110mm
Maximum Speed: 125km/h (78mph)

Chassis: pressed steel side members. Front and rear suspension comprising semi-elliptic springs and friction dampers
Dimensions: wheelbase 290cm (114in). Track 132cm (52in)
Brakes: four-wheel drum
The first MGs were based on Morris products, but the Mark II, which first appeared at the 1929 Motor Show, was the first MG to completely shed its Morris ancestry. It was heavier and more expensive than its predecessor, the Mark I, and was a more luxurious model generally; it had a sturdier frame, better brakes and a wider track.

JORDAN Speedway Eight

Country of Origin: USA
Date: 1930
Engine: Continental, eight vertical cylinders, in line; side valves; 114bhp
Gears: four-speed
Capacity: 5,180cc
Bore & Stroke: 85 × 114mm
Maximum Speed: 160km/h (100mph)
Chassis: front and rear suspension by semi-elliptic springs
Dimensions: Wheelbase over 365cm (144in)
Brakes: hydraulic, four-wheel
Body: aluminium; Sportsman sedan, or Ace roadster

Edward Jordan made cars from 1916 to 1930, the magnificent Speedway Eight being the last model the

company produced. It had clean, modern (for its time) bodywork of which there were two types offered – the Sportsman Sedan and the Ace roadster. It was a reliable, quiet, good-quality car, with Woodlite headlamps, aerofoil running boards and twin trumpet horns.

WOLSELEY Hornet

Country of Origin: Great Britain
Date: 1930
Engine: Morris Minor straight six; single ohc; one SU carburettor; 32bhp at 4,300rpm
Gears: three-speed manual
Capacity: 1,271cc
Bore & Stroke: 57 × 83mm
Maximum Speed: 95km/h (60mph)
Chassis: pressed steel side members. Front and rear suspension comprising semi-elliptic springs and hydraulic dampers

Dimensions: wheelbase 230cm (90.5in). Track 107cm (42in)

Brakes: four-wheel hydraulic drum

Sports-car purists tend to deny that the Hornet is a sports-car at all, but in the early 1930s it met the needs of many people who wanted an affordable fun car. Its square shape and over-long bonnet gave it a very unstylish appearance, but it had power, easy top-gear driving and good brakes. Hornets appeared frequently in sporting events at Brooklands, Donington and Shelsley Walsh.

MASERATI 8C-1100

Country of Origin: Italy
Date: 1931
Engine: eight vertical cyclinders in line; two valves
per cylinder; ohvs operated by two ohcs; Roots
supercharger; 100bhp at 5,500rpm
Gears: four-speed
Capacity: 1,078cc
Bore & Stroke: 51 × 66mm

Dimensions: Wheelbase 272 cm (107.25 in)
Maximum Speed: 185km/h (115mph)
Chassis: front and rear suspension by semi-elliptic springs
Body: two-seater
Won its class in the Mille Miglia in 1931 and 1932.

ALVIS TK 12/60

Country of Origin: Great Britain
Date: 1931/2
Engine: four-cylinders in line; pushrod ohv; two SU carburettors; 52bhp at 4,500rpm
Gears: four-speed
Capacity: 1,645cc
Bore & Stroke: 69 × 110mm
Maximum Speed: 121km/h (75mph)
Chassis: front and rear suspension by semi-elliptic springs

Dimensions: wheelbase 285cm (112in). Track 127cm (50in)

This was the last of a series of good, sound, cheaper and popular sports models built by Alvis in the 1920s and 1930s. It had very good brakes and was economical to run, having a fuel consumption of about 28 mpg. It was a developed version of the famous Alvis 12/50, one of the most famous vintage sports cars of all time.

BUGATTI Type 55

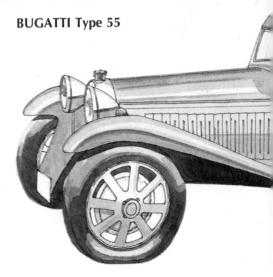

Country of Origin: France
Date: 1932
Engine: eight-cylinder, 2.3-litre; twin ohcs; two inclined valves per cylinder; 135bhp at 5,000rpm
Gears: four-speed
Capacity: 2,270cc
Bore & Stroke: 60 × 100mm
Maximum Speed: 185km/h (115mph)

Dimensions: wheelbase 274cm (108in)
Tyres: 48 × 12cm
Another extraordinary Bugatti car with acceleration in the order of 0–160km/h (0–100mph) in 43 seconds. It had a greater elegance of style than some of the other Bugatti models, with cutaway sides and long, flared wings and was generally a more refined machine altogether. Its performance, as to be expected from Bugatti, was excellent.

DUESENBERG Model J Roadster

Country of Origin: USA
Date: 1932
Engine: Lycoming straight eight; twin ohc; single twin choke carburettor; 250bhp at 4,250rpm
Gears: three-speed manual
Capacity: 6,882cc
Bore & Stroke: 95 × 121mm
Maximum Speed: 185km/h (115mph)
Chassis: pressed steel side members. Front and rear suspension by semi-elliptic springs and hydraulic dampers
Dimensions: wheelbase 362cm (142.5in) or 390cm (153.5in). Track 142cm (56in)

Brakes: four-wheel drum with hydraulic servo assistance. Transmission brake

This was one of America's most luxurious cars. It was a car designed to out-perform any other American car, the price being a secondary factor. Its enormous engine had more than twice the power of any other American car. It was followed in the series by the 320-hp SJ which had a centrifugal supercharger. The collapse of the Cord Corporation also spelt the end for Duesenberg.

SINGER Le Mans Nine

Country of Origin: Great Britain
Date: 1932
Engine: straight four; single ohc; twin carburettors; 45bhp at 5,500rpm
Gears: four-speed manual with synchromesh
Capacity: 972cc
Bore & Stroke: 60 × 86mm
Maximum Speed: 105km/h (65mph)
Chassis: pressed steel side members. Front and rear suspension comprising semi-elliptic leaf springs
Dimensions: wheelbase 231cm (91in).

Brakes: four-wheel Lockheed hydraulic drum
The Singer Le Mans Nine was the main rival to MG in the cheap sports-car market. Its performance was good and it had many notable successes in sports-car events both in Britain and Europe, such as the 1933 24-Hour Le Mans Race where it came in thirteenth place, running like clockwork throughout. In their day, the Le Mans two-seaters were among the most successful small sports cars produced in Britain.

DELAGE D8SS

Country of Origin: France
Date: 1933
Engine: straight eight; pushrod ohv; single carburettor; 110bhp at 3,500rpm
Gears: four-speed manual
Capacity: 4,060cc
Bore & Stroke: 77 × 109mm
Maximum Speed: 145km/h (90mph)
Chassis: pressed steel side members with cruciform bracing. Independent front suspension by transverse

leaf spring and wishbones. Rear suspension by semi-elliptic springs and dampers

Dimensions: wheelbase 330cm (130in). Track 150cm (59in)

Brakes: four-wheel drum

The D8 series were high-performance cars, but were not suitable for racing because they were too large and elegant. The D8SS (Sport Surbaissé) was only produced in small numbers; a further development of it, the D8SS-100, was very special, able to reach 160km/h (100mph). This car also broke several speed records at Montlhéry.

MG Magnette K3

Country of Origin: Great Britain
Date: 1933
Engine: straight six; single ohc; one SU carburettor with supercharger; 125bhp at 6,500rpm
Gears: four speed preselector
Capacity: 1,087cc
Bore & Stroke: 51 × 71mm
Chassis: pressed steel side members. Front and rear suspension comprised of semi-elliptic springs and friction dampers
Dimensions: wheelbase 239cm (94in).
Brakes: four-wheel drum

The Magnette K3 was the result of development work done originally on the 1930 Wolsey Hornet six-cylinder. Its first modifications resulted in the F-Type Magna with a 1,271cc engine. In 1932 the Magna was developed into the K1 Magnette saloon, which was immediately followed by the K2 two-seater and finally the supercharged K3 Magnette racer. This extraordinary car won its class in the 1933 Mille Miglia, and in the same year, driven by Tazio Nuvolari, was overall winner in the RAC Tourist Trophy at Ards. K3s rapidly developed a sound reputation as both competition cars and high-speed roadsters. The originals which survive are highly sought-after and very valuable.

FRAZER NASH TT Replica

Country of Origin: Great Britain
Date: 1934
Engine: Blackburne straight six, 1.5- or 1.65-litre; twin ohcs; two or three carburettors; 70 or 74bhp at 5,000rpm
Gears: four-speed manual
Capacity: 1,498cc (or 1667cc)
Bore & Stroke: 57 × 98mm (or 60 × 98mm)
Maximum Speed: above 130km/h (80mph)
Chassis: pressed steel side members. Front suspension by reversed quarter-elliptic springs. Rear suspension quarter-elliptic springs; friction dampers
Dimensions: wheelbase 259cm (102in) with optional 274cm (108in). Track (front) 122cm (48in); track (rear) 107cm (42in)

This model went through a variety of changes of engine, beginning with a Powerplus, superseded by the 1½-litre side-valve Anzani, the ohv Meadows and then, from 1934, the Gough ohc 1½-litre, four-cylinder unit. The six-cylinder Blackburne was the last of the line, since the days of chain-drive cars were over and after the war the more sophisticated models took over. The car was fast and easily controllable with extremely good cornering ability.

RAILTON

Country of Origin: Great Britain
Date: 1934
Engine: Hudson four-litre straight eight; side valves; one carburettor; 113bhp at 3,800rpm
Gears: Hudson three-speed, manual
Capacity: 4,010cc
Bore & Stroke: 75 × 113mm
Maximum Speed: 145km/h (90mph)
Chassis: pressed steel side members. Front suspension comprising radius arms, semi-elliptic leaf

springs and friction/hydraulic dampers. Rear suspension comprising semi-elliptic leaf springs and friction/hydraulic dampers

Dimensions: wheelbase 287cm (113in). Track 142cm (56in)

Brakes: mechanically operated four-wheel drum

The Railton was noted for its phenomenal acceleration and complete reliability. It could go from zero-to-80km/h (50mph) in a mere 7.2 seconds. It had a formidable power-to-weight ratio with a large, comparatively slow-revving engine coupled with a light frame and body. Although a standard road car, the Railton was a frequent winner at Brooklands and elsewhere.

87

RILEY Sprite

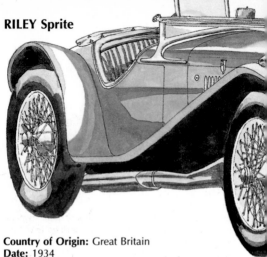

Country of Origin: Great Britain
Date: 1934
Engine: straight four; pushrod ohv; twin carburettors; 61bhp at 5,000rpm
Gears: four-speed manual; optional four-speed pre-selector
Capacity: 1,496cc
Bore & Stroke: 69 × 100mm
Maximum Speed: 140km/h (85mph)
Chassis: box-section pressed steel side members, underslung at rear. Front and rear suspension comprising of semi-elliptic leaf springs, friction dampers

Dimensions: wheelbase 248cm (97.5in). Track 122cm (48in)

Brakes: four-wheel rod-operated Girling drum

The engine of this handsome car was an enlarged version of the famous four-cylinder Nine engine, while the rest of the car was a direct descendent of the Riley MPH two-seater. The chassis was basically the same as in the MPH, with the addition of Girling brakes; the bodywork was extensively restyled, with elegant, curving wings and an unusual radiator cowling, with its 'fencer's mask' shape.

SQUIRE

Country of Origin: Great Britain
Date: 1934
Engine: Anzani straight four 1½-litre; twin ohc; one SU carburettor with Roots supercharger; 105bhp at 5,000rpm
Gears: separate Wilson four-speed preselector
Capacity: 1,496cc
Bore & Stroke: 69 × 120mm
Maximum Speed: 177km/h (110mph)
Chassis: pressed steel side members, cruciform bracing. Independent front and rear suspension by semi-elliptic leaf springs, hydraulic dampers
Dimensions: wheelbase 259cm (102in), or 312cm (123in). Track 137cm (54in)

Brakes: four-wheel drum
Body: Vanden Plas two-seater

The Squire was one of the most attractive and expensive sports cars ever built. Adrian Squire, its designer, was building to an ideal, not a method generally encouraging economy. It incorporated many features developed from racing practice, such as the Anzani engine which was worthy of a GP racing car and had twin water pumps. It had excellent roadholding and braking, and beautifully styled Vanden Plas bodywork. But sadly it was completely uncompetitive in price and the company was wound up in 1936.

VALE Special

Country of Origin: Great Britain
Date: 1934
Engine: Triumph Super Seven; 28bhp at 6,000rpm; one SU carburettor
Gears: four-speed manual
Capacity: 832cc
Bore & Stroke: 56.5 × 83mm
Maximum Speed: 96.5km/h (60mph)
Chassis: underslung at front and rear, with semi-elliptic springs anchored at one end, free to slide under stress
Dimensions: wheelbase 213cm (84in). Track 117cm (46in)
Tyres: 11.4 × 48cm

Brakes: hydraulic
Body: two- or four-seater
These neat little cars had enormous vogue in the 1930s, although the performance of some of the earlier models was rather disappointing. Its very low build ensured good roadholding and cornering abilities. They were very good high-speed touring cars and although their performance was not first class they collected many awards in sporting events between 1934–36.

AUBURN 851 Speedster

Country of Origin: USA
Date: 1935
Engine: Lycoming straight eight; side valves; single carburettor; Schwitzer-Cummins centrifugal supercharger; 148bhp at 4,000rpm
Gears: three-speed with Colombia two-speed rear axle
Capacity: 4,596cc
Bore & Stroke: 78 × 121mm
Maximum Speed: 160km/h (100mph)
Chassis: pressed steel side members. Front and rear suspension by semi-elliptic springs

Dimensions: wheelbase 323cm (127in). Track (front) 150cm (59in); track (rear) 157cm (62in)
Brakes: Lockheed hydraulic

The Auburn was one of the few pre-World War II American sports cars and one of the best known. It was a large-bodied car, designed by Buerig and updated for the 1935 version, which included the famous white-wall tyres. The weight of the car meant it was steady at high speeds while the engine ensured that high speeds could be reached. The Auburn disappeared with the collapse of the Auburn-Cord-Duesenberg Corporation.

BUGATTI T57S

Country of Origin: France
Date: 1935
Engine: straight eight; twin ohcs; single carburettor; 170bhp at 5,500rpm; supercharged
Gears: four-speed manual
Capacity: 3,257cc
Bore & Stroke: 72 × 100mm
Chassis: pressed steel side members. Suspension by semi-elliptic front springs, reversed quarter-elliptic rears; hydraulic dampers

Dimensions: wheelbase 298cm (117.5in). Track 135cm (53in)
Brakes: four-wheel drum, mechanically operated
This was the sports version of the T57 of 1934. It had a shorter, lower chassis with the rear axle passing through it, and the engine was set lower with dry-sump lubrication and raised compression. One of its distinguishing features was the beautiful horse shoe-shaped radiator.

DELAHAYE Type 135

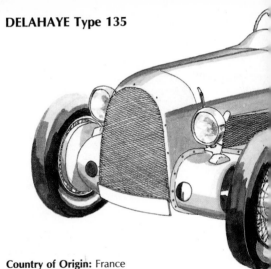

Country of Origin: France
Date: 1935
Engine: six-cylinder, 3½-litre; pushrod ohv; single or triple carburettors; 130bhp at 3,850rpm
Gears: four-speed manual with synchromesh; optional Cotal electro-magnetic
Capacity: 3,558cc
Bore & Stroke: 84 × 107mm
Chassis: box-section side members. Independent front suspension comprising transverse leaf spring,

swing links and radius arms. Rear suspension comprising semi-elliptic springs; friction and hydraulic dampers

Dimensions: wheelbase 295cm (116in). Track (front) 140cm (55in); track (rear) 147cm (58in)

Brakes: four-wheel Bendix mechanical drum; with servo assistance

One of the most famous Delahaye models, along with the 3.2-litre Coupé des Alpes. It had a wide choice of types of bodywork, its engine had coil ignition and air cleaners; it was flexible, fast and reliable and won at Monte Carlo in 1937 and 1939.

FIAT Tipo 508S

Country of Origin: Italy
Date: 1935
Engine: straight four; pushrod ohv; one Zenith carburettor; 36bhp at 4,400rpm
Gears: four-speed, close ratio manual; synchromesh
Capacity: 995cc
Bore & Stroke: 65 × 75mm
Maximum Speed: 116km/h (72mph)
Chassis: pressed steel side members with cruciform bracing. Front and rear suspension by semi-elliptic springs and friction dampers
Dimensions: wheelbase 233cm (91.5in). Track (front) 119cm (47in); track (rear) 121cm (47.5in)
Brakes: four-wheel hydraulic drum

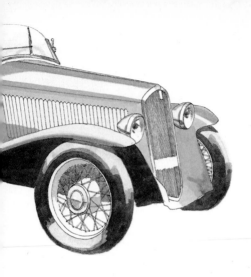

The performance of this perky little model was on a par with the Lancia Aprilia, a much more august vehicle. It was a variant of the famous Fiat Ballila, and of the 113,000 produced, 1,000 were these sports versions. They did well in sports-car racing up to 1,100cc. The Tipo 508S was about the only continental sports car to challenge the British-built small cars. It sold well and raced in many European countries.

RILEY Imp

Country of Origin: Great Britain
Date: 1935
Engine: straight four; pushrod ohv; twin SU carburettors; 41bhp at 5,000rpm
Gears: four-speed manual; optional 'Preselectagear' transmission
Capacity: 1,089cc
Bore & Stroke: 60.3 × 95.2mm
Maximum Speed: 115km/h (70mph)
Chassis: box-section side members with cross-bracing, underslung at rear. Front and rear suspension by semi-elliptic leaf springs, friction dampers

Dimensions: wheelbase 230cm (90.5in). Track 121cm (47.5in)
Brakes: four-wheel drum
Body: two-seater; fold-down windscreen
The final variant of the original Riley Nine, the Imp was a very neat and pretty car with a rounded tail and flared wings. These racy styling characteristics were belied by its performance which did not quite live up to its appearance. It was popular for rallying but lacked the power for racing.

BMW 328

Country of Origin: Germany
Date: 1936
Engine: six-cylinder 2-litre; ohv in V-form; ohc; three Solex downdraught 30 JF carburettors; 80 hp at 5,000rpm
Gears: four-speed
Capacity: 1,971cc
Bore & Stroke: 66 × 96mm
Maximum Speed: 150km/h (93mph)
Chassis: tubular. Independent front suspension by transverse leaf springs. Rear suspension, live axle with longitudinal leaf springs
Dimensions: wheelbase 240cm (94.5in). Track (front) 115.3cm (45.4in); track (rear) 122cm (48in)

Steering: rack-and-pinion
Brakes: four-wheel hydraulic
The most famous BMW six-cylinder model, this car
won many races with drivers including Prince Bira
and Dick Seaman. The first six-cylinder BMW was a
1,173cc which appeared in 1933, designed by Fritz
Fiedler. By 1936 it had the capacity to perform like a
twin ohc engine without having to build such an
engine to a realistic production price. It was very
reliable, and set standards of precision, roadholding
and cornering which had never been seen in Germany before.

.ISS Grand Sport

Country of Origin: France
Date: 1936
Engine: six vertical cylinders, in line; pushrod operated ohv; twin Solex or Stromberg carburettors; 120bhp at 3,800rpm
Gears: four-speed
Capacity: 3,485cc
Bore & Stroke: 86 × 100mm
Maximum Speed: 175km/h (110mph)
Chassis: pressed steel side members with cruciform bracing. Front and rear suspension by semi-elliptic springs and hydraulic dampers

Dimensions: wheelbase 279cm (110in). Track 142cm (56in)
Brakes: Lockheed hydraulic
Body: coupé or sedan
The 1936 Hotchkiss was designed by Bertarione who joined Hotchkiss from Sunbeam-Talbot-Darracq in 1935. It was an outstandingly good car in terms of reliability and roadholding and had excellent steering and brakes. The Grand Sport continued its successful career after the war and won at Monte Carlo in 1949 and 1950.

LAGONDA Rapier

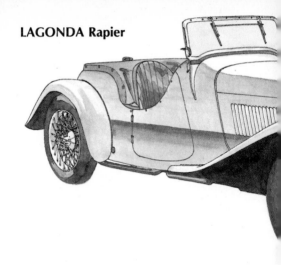

Country of Origin: Great Britain
Date: 1936
Engine: four-cylinder; ohv operated by twin ohcs;
46bhp at 4,500rpm two SU carburettors
Gears: Wilson, preselector, four-speed
Capacity: 1,104cc
Bore & Stroke: 62.5 × 90mm
Maximum Speed: 145km/h (90mph)

Chassis: front and rear suspension comprising semi-elliptic leaf springs
Dimensions: wheelbase 231cm (91in).
Brakes: Girling
The Rapier was a small, high-grade sports car and was very popular during the late 1930s. It had beautifully styled bodywork and a reputation for very good performance. The Rapier was one of the first cars to be fitted with Girling brakes.

MERCEDES-BENZ 540K

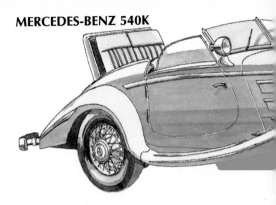

Country of Origin: Germany
Date: 1936
Engine: eight cylinders, in line; two pushrod ohvs per cylinder. Single up-draught Mercedes-Benz carburettor with optionally engaged Roots-type supercharger; 115bhp (or 180bhp supercharged) at 3,600rpm
Gears: four-speed manual with synchromesh (except on first gear)
Capacity: 5,401cc
Bore & Stroke: 88 × 111mm
Maximum Speed: 169km/h (105mph)
Chassis: separate pressed steel box-section frame with box-section bracing. Independent front suspen-

sion comprising coil spring and wishbones. Independent rear suspension comprising swing axles and double coil springs (one in front, one behind the half-shaft line)

Dimensions: wheelbase 329cm (129.5in). Track (front) 151cm (59.5in); track (rear) 150cm (59in)

Steering: worm-type

Brakes: four-wheel hydraulic drum, with Bosch vacuum servo assistance

This impressive, exclusive car was the final flowering of the 370K of 1931. These sports-tourers of the 1930s were the most glamorous of all Daimler-Benz products and the 540K was one of the fastest German road cars in the pre-war period.

LAGONDA Rapide LG45

Country of Origin: Great Britain
Date: 1937
Engine: Meadows straight six; pushrod ohv; twin SU carburettors; 130bhp at 4,000rpm
Gears: separate four-speed manual
Capacity: 4,453cc
Bore & Stroke: 88.5 × 120.6mm
Chassis: pressed steel side members. Suspension front and rear comprising semi-elliptic springs and hydraulic dampers

Dimensions: wheelbase 312cm (123in). Track 147cm (58in)

Brakes: four-wheel Girling; servo assisted

Designed by W.O. Bentley, the LG45 was successor to the M45 for a short time before being superseded by newer models. Like its predecessor, this magnificent car had long, elegant wings, a handsome, vertically slatted radiator and a new feature was its outside exhaust pipes.

ALFA ROMEO 8C 2900B

Country of Origin: Italy
Date: 1938
Engine: straight eight; twin Roots-type super-chargers; ohv operated by two ohcs; twin carburettors; 180bhp at 5,200rpm
Gears: four-speed manual transaxle
Capacity: 2,905cc
Bore & Stroke: 68 × 100mm
Maximum Speed: 225km/h (140mph)
Chassis: welded box-section side members. Independent suspension with trailing links and coil springs in unit with hydraulic dampers at front and

transverse leaf spring at rear with combined friction and hydraulic dampers.

Dimensions: wheelbase 279cm (110in) or 300cm (118in); track 135cm (53in)

Body: spyder, with light alloy tube framing supporting light alloy panelling

This car was one of the world's fastest catalogued cars of its time. It was part of a series which began after the reorganisation of the Alfa Romeo company in 1933 which reflected a change of emphasis away from the small, rich elite towards a larger market.

JENSEN

Country of Origin: Great Britain
Date: 1938
Engine: Nash straight eight; 3½-litre; 120bhp at 3,500rpm; ohvs; dual ignition; two SU carburettors
Gears: six-speed
Capacity: 4,205cc
Bore & Stroke: 79.3 × 107.9mm
Maximum Speed: above 145km/h (90mph)
Chassis: front and rear suspension by transverse springing

Dimensions: wheelbase 320cm (126in). Track 150cm (59in)

The 1938 Jensen continued the Jensen tradition of finely crafted, striking bodywork, good roadholding abilities and fine performance. This model had several interesting features including dual ignition and a dual-ratio back axle which gave the car six forward speeds.

SS 100

Country of Origin: Great Britain
Date: 1939
Engine: 3½-litre, six cylinders in line; ohv operated by pushrods; twin SU carburettors; 125bhp at 4,500rpm
Gears: four-speed
Capacity: 3,485cc
Bore & Stroke: 82 × 110mm
Maximum Speed: 163km/h (101mph)

Chassis: box-section frame with cruciform bracing. Front and rear suspension semi-elliptic springs
Dimensions: wheelbase 264cm (104in). Track (front) 133cm (52in); track (rear) 137cm (54in)
Brakes: Girling rod
The SS 100 sports car was the peak of Sir William Lyons' previous achievements. It was an extremely beautiful model and had good performance on both road and track, distinguishing itself in rallies, sprints and other sporting events.

FRAZER NASH 2-litre Le Mans Replica

Country of Origin: Great Britain
Date: 1948
Engine: Bristol-BMW straight six; cross-pushrod ohv;
three Solex carburettors, 125bhp at 5,500rpm
Gears: four-speed manual
Capacity: 1,971cc
Bore & Stroke: 66 × 96mm
Maximum Speed: 185km/h (115mph)
Chassis: welded tubular side members. Independent
front suspension comprising transverse leaf spring
and wishbones. Rear suspension by longitudinal
torsion bars and A-bracket, hydraulic dampers

Dimensions: wheelbase 244cm (96in). Track 122cm (48in)
Steering: rack-and-pinion
Brakes: four-wheel hydraulic drum

Won the 1951 Targa Florio to make the Frazer Nash the only British car to have won a race on the Sicilian circuit. The Bristol-BMW engine, a developed version of the previous BMW Type 328 engine was used in all post-war Frazer-Nash models up until 1952.

Country of Origin: Great Britain
Date: 1948
Engine: Singer straight four, 1½-litre; single ohc; twin SU carburettors; 65bhp at 4,800rpm
Gears: four-speed manual, with synchromesh
Capacity: 1,496cc
Bore & Stroke: 68 × 103mm
Maximum Speed: 145km/h (90mph)
Chassis: pressed steel side members. Front suspension, quarter-elliptic springs; rear suspension, semielliptic springs; hydraulic dampers
Dimensions: wheelbase 263cm (103.5in). Track (front) 122cm (48in); track (rear) 114cm (45in)
Brakes: four-wheel drum

The history of this neat little car spans both the pre- and post-war years, and during both periods it did very well in races and rallies. In the years 1937–39 it

tackled the 24-hour Le Mans, finishing second in its class in 1938 and winning its class in 1939. Production was quite slow, and by September 1939 only 36 cars had been built. In the post-war period, the model changed very little, and by the time production ceased in 1955 only 240 HRGs had ever been made.

JAGUAR XK120

Country of Origin: Great Britain
Date: 1949
Engine: straight six; twin ohc; twin SU carburettors; 160bhp at 5,000rpm
Gears: four-speed manual
Capacity: 3,442cc
Bore & Stroke: 83 × 106mm
Maximum Speed: 201km/h (125mph)
Chassis: box-frame. Independent front suspension comprising wishbones, torsion bars, dampers. Rear suspension by live axle, semi-elliptic springs and dampers

Dimensions: wheelbase 259cm (102in). Track (front) 129cm (51in); track (rear) 127cm (50in)
Brakes: four-wheel drum
The XK120 took the sports-car world by storm when it appeared at the London Motor Show in 1948. It was unveiled at the same time as the XK100, and demand for it was so great that the XK100 never went into production. The name XK120 was meant to indicate that the car was capable of 120mph (193km/h), and in fact it was recorded as reaching 125mph (201km/h).

MORGAN Plus Four

Country of Origin: Great Britain
Date: 1950
Engine: Standard Vanguard straight four; 2.1-litre; pushrod ohv; one carburettor; 68bhp at 4,000rpm
Gears: separate four-speed manual
Capacity: 2,088cc
Bore & Stroke: 85 × 92mm
Chassis: Z-section side members. Independent front suspension comprising vertical sliding pillars, coil springs and dampers. Rear suspension comprising rigid axle, semi-elliptic leaf springs and dampers

Dimensions: wheelbase 244cm (96in). Track 114cm (45in)

Brakes: four-wheel drum

The Morgan Plus Four was an improved post-war version when the ohv Standard 10 unit was replaced by the 2.1-litre Vanguard engine. It had a wider track and body than previous versions but remained a compact little two-seater with the traditional fine Morgan performance and strong road-holding abilities. It was very successful as a competition car.

ALLARD J2X

Country of Origin: Great Britain
Date: 1951
Engine: Mercury V-8; Ardun ohc; two Solex carburettors; 140bhp at 4,000rpm
Gears: three-speed manual
Capacity: 3,917cc

Bore & Stroke: 81 × 95.2mm
Maximum Speed: 175km/h (110mph)
Chassis: ladder frame. Independent front suspension by split axles, radius arms, coil springs and dampers. De Dion rear suspension, coil springs and dampers
Dimensions: wheelbase 254cm (100in). Track 142cm (56in)
Brakes: four-wheel drum

This was the archetypal Allard car with its spare alloy body and powerful acceleration. The standard engine was the Mercury, but Allard also sold cars to American customers without engines since the chassis would take most V-8 engines. J2s with Cadillac engines were unbeatable in US sports-car racing for a short time in the 1950s.

PORSCHE 356

Country of Origin: Germany
Date: 1951
Engine: VW horizontally opposed, four-cylinder; pushrod ohv; two Solex carburettors; 40bhp at 4,000rpm
Gears: four-speed manual, without synchromesh
Capacity: 1,086cc
Bore & Stroke: 73.5 × 64mm
Maximum Speed: 140km/h (80mph)
Chassis: pressed steel. Independent front suspension, upper and lower trailing arms, transverse torsion bars. Rear suspension, swing axles, trailing arms, transverse torsion bars

Dimensions: wheelbase 210cm (82.7in). Track (front) 129cm (50.8in). Track (rear) 125cm (49in)
Steering: worm-and-peg
Brakes: ATE-Lockheed hydraulic drum
Body: coupé, cabriolet

The 356 had a rear-mounted, air-cooled VW engine. The series remained basically the same from 1951 to 1964. Porsche rapidly made its name in racing, sprinting, hillclimbing and rallying all over the world. The 356s had a very fine power-to-weight ratio which complemented their high-speed cornering capacity. They were enormously reliable, a tradition which Porsche has continued to this day.

ASTON MARTIN DB2/4

Country of Origin: Great Britain
Date: 1953
Engine: straight six; twin ohcs; twin SU carburettors; 125bhp at 5,000rpm
Gears: four-speed manual
Capacity: 2,580cc
Bore & Stroke: 78 × 90mm
Maximum Speed: 185km/h (115mph)
Chassis: multi-tube spaceframe. Independent front suspension comprising trailing links, coil springs, anti-roll bar and dampers. Rear suspension comprising, twin radius arms, Panhard rod, coil springs and dampers

Dimensions: wheelbase 251cm (99in). Track 137cm (54in)

Brakes: four-wheel Girling drum

The prefix DB stands for David Brown, whose company had taken over Aston Martin in 1947. The DB series continued with, among others, the DB3 of 1954, a sports-racer actively promoted in racing by the company and the DBR, which won the 1959 Le Mans and the Sports Car Constructors' Championship.

133

AUSTIN HEALEY 100

Country of Origin: Great Britain
Date: 1953
Engine: Austin A90 Atlantic; straight four; pushrod ohv; twin SU carburettors; 90bhp at 4,000rpm
Gears: three-speed manual with overdrive
Capacity: 2,660cc
Bore & Stroke: 87.3 × 111.1mm
Maximum Speed: 164km/h (102mph)
Chassis: ladder-type; independent front suspension by wishbones, coil springs and dampers; rear suspension comprising of live axle, semi-elliptic springs and dampers

Dimensions: wheelbase 234cm (92in); track 126cm (49.5in)
Tyres: 15 × 38cm
Brakes: four-wheel drum

This car was the star of the 1952 London Motor Show and over the next 15 years nearly 74,000 cars were produced. The Austin-Healey name was subsequently carried by the 'Frog-Eye' Sprites of which nearly 50,000 were made. In 1953 long-distance record-breaking attempts it achieved 198km/h (123mph) over 12 hours, and subsequently 166km/h (103mph) over 30 hours. The model did well in amateur speed events. In 1956 the four-cylinder power unit was replaced by the six-cylinder unit, but performance was not noticeably improved.

BENTLEY R-Type Continental

Country of Origin: Great Britain
Date: 1953
Engine: Rolls-Royce, six-cylinder, 4.6-litre; bhp not known; overhead inlet side exhaust; two SU carburettors
Gears: four-speed, with synchromesh
Capacity: 4,566cc
Bore & Stroke: 92 × 114.3mm
Maximum Speed: 190km/h (120mph)
Chassis: front suspension by coil springs. Rear suspension by semi-elliptic springs

Dimensions: wheelbase 305cm (120in). Track 148.5cm (58.5in)
Tyres: 16.5 × 40.5cm
Brakes: servo, with hydro-mechanical actuation
The elegant fastback Bentley R-Type Continental was the fastest four-seater closed car of its time. It had economical fuel consumption and a cruising speed of 150–160km/h (95–100mph). There was a convertible version by Park Ward, but this was one of a number of very specialised bodies available and H.J. Mulliner's fastback remained the most common version.

TRIUMPH TR2

Country of Origin: Great Britain
Date: 1953
Engine: Standard Vanguard straight four; pushrod-ohv; SU carburettors; 90bhp at 5,000rpm
Gears: four-speed manual with optional overdrive
Capacity: 1,991cc
Bore & Stroke: 83 × 92mm
Maximum Speed: 160km/h (100mph)
Chassis: steel. Independent front suspension comprising coil springs, wishbones, dampers. Rear suspension comprising live axle, leaf springs, dampers

Dimensions: wheelbase 224cm (88in). Track (front) 114cm (45in); track (rear) 116cm (45.5in)

Brakes: four-wheel drum

The TR2 was a relatively low-cost vehicle, using components from existing models as far as possible. It was a sturdy rather than elegant or stylish model and was both economical and reliable. However, only 8,628 were produced before it was replaced by the TR3. TR2s won many competition events – such as the Tourist Trophy and the Alpine Rally, both 1954 victories. A TR2 also finished fifteenth out of 18 finishers at Le Mans in the same year.

MERCEDES Type 300SL

Country of Origin: Germany
Date: 1954
Engine: six cylinders, in line; two ohvs per cylinder; single ohc; Bosch direct fuel injection; 215bhp at 5,800rpm
Gears: four-speed, all synchromesh, manual
Capacity: 2,996cc
Bore & Stroke: 85 × 88mm
Chassis: separate multi-tubular spaceframe. Independent front suspension by coil springs and wishbones. Independent rear suspension by coil springs, swing axles and radius arms. Telescopic dampers
Dimensions: wheelbase 240cm (94.5in). Track (front) 140cm (55in) track (rear) 145cm (57in)

140

The great feature of the 300SL was its futuristic (for the time) coupé body with the uplift 'gull-wing' doors. A technical novelty was the Bosch fuel injection – the 300SL was the first ever production car on sale with fuel injection as standard. It was one of the fastest road cars of the 1950s. There were problems with the gullwing doors however, they made the car difficult to get in and out of and needed a lot of space in which to open and close. They were abandoned for the 300SL Roadster style in 1957.

AC Ace-Bristol

Country of Origin: Great Britain
Date: 1956
Engine: Bristol straight-six 2-litre; pushrod ohv; three Solex carburettors; 140bhp
Gears: four-speed manual, with optional overdrive
Capacity: 1,971cc
Bore & Stroke: 66 × 96mm
Maximum Speed: 193km/h (120mph)
Chassis: tubular frame, designed by John Tojeiro. Independent suspension front and rear by wishbones, leaf springs and dampers
Dimensions: wheelbase 229cm (90in); track 127cm (50in)
Tyres: 14 × 40.6cm
Brakes: disc front/Girling hydraulic drum at rear

The chassis frame was designed by John Tojeiro. The Bristol engine was derived from the BMW 328. In 1957 the car was entered in the Le Mans 24-Hours race and came tenth in general classification. It also came second in the 1,500–2,000cc class, driven by Rudd and Bolton. In 1959 Whiteaway and Turner drove an Ace into seventh place overall at Le Mans behind four Ferraris and an Aston Martin. Carroll Shelby based his Ford V-8 conversion – the Shelby Cobra – on the Ace.

LOTUS Eleven

Country of Origin: Great Britain
Date: 1956
Engine: Coventry-Climax straight four; single ohc;
twin SU carburettors; 84bhp at 6,800rpm
Gears: four-speed manual
Capacity: 1,098cc
Bore & Stroke: 72.4 × 66.6mm
Chassis: spaceframe. Independent front suspension
comprising wishbones, coil springs, anti-roll bar,
dampers. Rear suspension comprising de Dion axle,
coil springs, dampers

Dimensions: wheelbase 224cm (88in). Track (front) 115cm (45.5in); track (rear) 119cm (47in)
Brakes: four-wheel disc
The Lotus Eleven was the fourth in a series of path-breaking sports-car racers produced by Colin Chapman. It was a smooth, sleek-bodied car with a faired headrest. Graham Hill began his racing career in an Eleven and Stirling Moss broke several class records at Monza in one.

MORGAN 4/4 Series II

Country of Origin: Great Britain
Date: 1956
Engine: Ford straight four; side valves; one Solex carburettor; 36bhp at 4,000rpm
Gears: three speed manual, separate
Capacity: 1,172cc
Bore & Stroke: 63.5 × 92.5mm
Maximum Speed: 121km/h (75mph)
Chassis: Z-section side members. Independent front suspension by vertical sliding pillars, coil springs, dampers. Rear suspension comprising rigid axle, semi-elliptic leaf spring, dampers

146

Dimensions: wheelbase 244cm (96in). Track 114cm (45in)
Brakes: four-wheel drum

The 4/4 originally appeared in 1936 as Morgan's first four-wheeler and continued through until 1949. It was revived in 1955 in Series II form with a Ford engine. There were various updates and improvements including quick-release wire wheels (optional) and disc brakes (from 1960 onwards). The bodywork remained much the same as it was before the war, although it was improved slightly with the addition of a curved radiator and a more sloping tail.

147

ALFA ROMEO 2000 Spider

Country of Origin: Italy
Date: 1958
Engine: four-cylinders; 2-litre; twin ohcs; two horizontal dual-throat 44PHH Solex carburettors; 115bhp at 5,800rpm
Gears: five-speed
Capacity: 1,975cc
Bore & Stroke: 84.5 × 88mm
Maximum Speed: 177km/h (110mph)
Chassis: front suspension by wishbones, coil springs, telescopic dampers and anti-roll bar. Rear suspension by coil springs and rigid axle
Dimensions: wheelbase 158.5cm (98.5in)

One of Alfa Romeo's models aimed at a wider, cheaper, less specialised market. This robust and handsome car was capable of cruising along at touring speeds and was also capable of exhilarating performance when required. It could go from 0–97km/h (0–60mph) in 14.2 seconds. Looking almost identical to the famous Giuletta Spider, it could be distinguished by the two air intakes on top of the bonnet. As with all Alfa Romeos, its roadholding and performance were excellent.

LISTER-JAGUAR

Country of Origin: Great Britain
Date: 1958
Engine: Jaguar straight six; twin ohcs; Weber carburettors; 254bhp at 6,300rpm
Gears: four-speed manual
Capacity: 2,986cc
Bore & Stroke: 76.5 × 83mm
Chassis: tubular. Independent front suspension comprising wishbones, coil springs, dampers, anti-roll bar. Rear suspension comprising de Dion tube, radius arms, coil springs, dampers

Dimensions: wheelbase 230cm (90.5in). Track (front) 136cm (53.5in); track (rear) 140cm (55in)
Steering: rack-and-pinion
Brakes: Girling, four-wheel disc
This sports-racing car is considered by some to be the definitive Lister model. It had a very aggressive appearance with prominent wheel arches. These cars appeared in many racing events internationally and built up a fairly successful record. Fewer than 40 were ever built.

LOTUS Seven S3

Country of Origin: Great Britain
Date: 1958
Engine: Ford straight four; pushrod ohv; single Weber carburettor; 84bhp at 6,000rpm
Gears: four-speed manual
Capacity: 1,598cc
Bore & Stroke: 80.97 × 77.62mm
Maximum Speed: 174km/h (108mph)
Chassis: tubular. Independent front suspension comprising wishbones, coil springs, dampers. Rear suspension comprising live axle, radius arms, coil springs, dampers

Dimensions: wheelbase 218cm (86in). Track 124cm (49in)
Brakes: front/disc; rear/drum

The Seven was initially sold as a kit car, which enabled buyers to avoid certain taxes. Produced by Colin Chapman, the car slowly evolved over many years, surviving into the 1980s. It would have been discontinued much earlier by Lotus, but Caterham Cars bought the rights in 1973 and continued to supply a small number every year.

DAIMLER SP250

Country of Origin: Great Britain
Date: 1959
Engine: 90-degree V-8; pushrod ohv; twin SU carburettors; 140bhp at 5,800rpm
Gears: four-speed manual (optional three-speed automatic)
Capacity: 2,548cc
Bore & Stroke: 76.2 × 69.9mm
Maximum Speed: 190km/h (120mph)
Chassis: ladder frame. Independent front suspension by wishbones and coil springs. Rear suspension by rigid axle and semi-elliptic springs, hydraulic dampers

Dimensions: wheelbase 239cm (94in). Track (front) 128cm (50.5in); track (rear) 122cm (48in)
Brakes: four-wheel disc
This was an unusual vehicle from a company noted for its saloons and limousines. The chassis flexed to an extraordinary extent on the early cars and was corrected in 1961 when the specification for bodywork was modified. The resin-bonded glass fibre body was a mixture of sleek and rounded shapes which worked uneasily together but the engine was quiet and economical. Despite its popularity, the SP250 was phased out in 1964.

MG MGA

Country of Origin: Great Britain
Date: 1959
Engine: straight four; pushrod ohv; twin SU carburettors; 75bhp at 5,300rpm
Gears: four-speed manual
Capacity: 1,588cc
Bore & Stroke: 75.4 × 89mm
Chassis: unitary with steel body. Independent front suspension by wishbones, coil springs and dampers. Rear suspension by live axle, semi-elliptic leaf springs and dampers

Dimensions: wheelbase 239cm (94in). Track (front) 121cm (47.5in); track (rear) 123cm (48.5in)
Brakes: front/disc, rear/drum
This was the first MG sports car to adopt modern styling. It was a well-balanced car with almost 50/50 weight distribution. A wire wheel option was available. It was entered in racing events but after several accidents went into rallying instead. It ran at Le Mans in 1959–61, winning the 2-litre class in 1960. Over 100,000 were built, but competition lead to a sales Slump and it was discontinued in 1962.

LOTUS Elite

Country of Origin: Great Britain
Date: 1960
Engine: Coventry-Climax straight four; single ohc;
SU carburettor; 75bhp at 6,100rpm
Gears: BMC, four-speed manual
Capacity: 1,216cc
Bore & Stroke: 76.2 × 66.6mm
Maximum Speed: 180km/h (110mph)
Chassis: glass fibre-reinforced plastic monocoque.
Independent front suspension comprising wish-
bones, coil springs, dampers, anti-roll bar. Indepen-
dent rear suspension comprising radius arms, coil
springs, dampers
Dimensions: wheelbase 224cm (88in). Track (front)
119cm (47in); track (rear) 123cm (48.5in)

Brakes: four-wheel disc
Body: fixed-head coupé

This pretty and promising car proved to be a loss-maker for the manufacturers within a short time of its appearance. The body structure was subject to fatigue cracks which led to complaints from customers. However, in 1959, the Elite won the 1,300cc class at Nürburgring, and at Le Mans it won every year from 1959 to 1964. The surviving Lotus Elites are now very much collectors' items.

Country of Origin: Great Britain
Date: 1960
Engine: Coventry-Climax straight four; single ohc; twin SU carburettors; 75bhp at 6,000rpm
Gears: four-speed manual
Capacity: 1,098cc
Bore & Stroke: 72.4 × 66.6mm
Maximum Speed: 160km/h (100mph)
Chassis: tubular. Independent front suspension comprising wishbones, coil springs, dampers, anti-roll bar. Rear suspension comprising live axle, longitudinal torsion bars, radius arms, dampers

Dimensions: wheelbase 204cm (80.5in). Track (front) 116cm (45.5in), track (rear) 114cm (45in)
Brakes: front/disc; rear/drum
Body: glass fibre shell. Two-seater

These cars were part of a series of limited-production sports cars built by John Turner over a period of about eight years. The Coventry-Climax engine was introduced as an alternative to the BMC A-series unit in 1960. Its acceleration was comparable to the MGA and roadholding was good. Turners developed a good competition reputation and continued racing for several years after production ceased in 1966.

AC Cobra 289

Country of Origin: USA
Date: 1962
Engine: Ford 90-degree V-8; pushrod ohv; Ford carburettor; 271bhp at 6,000rpm
Gears: four-speed manual
Capacity: 4,727cc
Bore & Stroke: 101.6 × 72.9mm
Maximum Speed: 220km/h (135mph)
Chassis: tubular. Independent suspension front and rear, by wishbones, coil springs and dampers
Dimensions: wheelbase 229cm (90)in); front track 138cm (54.5in); rear track 137cm (54in)
Brakes: four-wheel disc
Body: Ferrari Barchetta-derived shell
Cobras 289s were placed fourth at Le Mans in 1964 and 1966. Later variations were the Cobra 427 with

a 7-litre engine with Frua bodywork and, in 1967 a 7016cc Ford V-8 was fitted and the model was then designated the 428, which remained available until 1973. The 4.7-litre Cobra was a phenomenal package, although in competition races its cornering abilities were found to be hair-raising, and the story got around that drivers would shut their eyes and hope! The 289 could go from 0–97km/h (0–60mph) in just 5.5 seconds. Production ceased in 1968.

AUSTIN HEALEY Sprite Mk II

Country of Origin: Great Britain
Date: 1962
Engine: straight four; pushrod ohv; twin SU carburettors; 56bhp at 5,750rpm
Gears: four-speed manual
Capacity: 1,098cc
Bore & Stroke: 64.6 × 83.7mm
Maximum Speed: 145km/h (90mph)
Chassis: steel monocoque. Independent front suspension by wishbones, coil springs and dampers. Rear suspension by live axle, quarter-elliptic springs and dampers

Dimensions: wheelbase 203cm (80in). Track (front) 120cm (47in); track (rear) 114cm (45in)
Tyres: 13.2 × 33cm
Brakes: front/disc, rear/drum
Originally produced in 1958 as an economical fun car, the 'frog-eyed' Sprite rapidly gained popularity as a club racer, and in late 1962 a more powerful model was produced to cater for this market. The Sprite Mk II became a well-known competitor in events throughout the 1960s.

FERRARI 250GTO

Country of Origin: Italy
Date: 1962
Engine: 60-degree V-12; single ohc per bank; Weber carburettors; 300bhp at 7,200rpm
Gears: five-speed manual
Capacity: 2,953cc
Bore & Stroke: 73 × 58.8mm
Chassis: multi-tubular with large-section side members. Independent front suspension comprising wishbones, coil springs, dampers and anti-roll bar. Rear suspension by live axle radius rods, half-elliptic leaf springs and dampers
Dimensions: wheelbase 240cm (94.5in). Track 135cm (53in)

Brakes: four-wheel disc
The 250GTO was the last of the Ferrari front-engined competition cars, the previous GT models going back to the mid-1950s when Ferrari began to take GT racing seriously. The GTO (the 'O' stood for *omologato*, homologated) was developed to overcome problems with the GT models, better stability at high speeds being one problem. The dry-sump engine facilitated a lower nose-line, and rear spoilers were also fitted. During its 1962 season the GTO came second and third at Le Mans.

TRIUMPH Spitfire MK I

Country of Origin: Great Britain
Date: 1962
Engine: straight four; pushrod ohv; twin SU carburettors; 63bhp at 5,750rpm
Gears: four-speed manual, with synchromesh
Capacity: 1,147cc
Bore & Stroke: 69.3 × 76mm
Maximum Speed: 145km/h (90mph)
Chassis: backbone frame. Independent front suspension comprising double wishbones, coil springs, anti-roll bar. Rear suspension comprising swing axles, transverse leaf spring, radius rods, dampers

Dimensions: wheelbase 211cm (83in). Track (front) 125cm (49in); track (rear) 122cm (48in)
Steering: rack-and-pinion
Brakes: front/disc; rear/drum
Body: two-seater, styled by Michelotti
The Spitfire was developed from the successful Herald saloon to fill the gap in the market for a small-capacity, inexpensive sporting car. Mechanically it was essentially the same as the Herald, and could reach 80km/h (50mph) from rest in about 12 seconds.

MG MGB

Country of Origin: Great Britain
Date: 1963
Engine: straight four; pushrod ohv; twin SU carburettors; 95bhp at 5,400rpm
Gears: four-speed manual
Capacity: 1,798cc
Bore & Stroke: 80.3 × 89mm
Maximum Speed: 175km/h (110mph)

Chassis: integral with body. Independent front suspension comprising wishbones, coil springs, dampers. Rear suspension by live axle, semi-elliptic leaf springs, dampers

Dimensions: wheelbase 200cm (78.5in). Track 125cm (49in)

Brakes: front/disc; rear/drum

Body: two-seater roadster

The MGB was a handsome model which retained its basic shape until 1980 when MG was wound up by its parent company, British Leyland. Even in 1980, although old-fashioned and long-obsolescent, there was still a large demand for the car.

CHEVROLET Corvette 'Stingray'

Country of Origin: USA
Date: 1964
Engine: straight six; pushrod ohv; Rochester carburettor; 360bhp at 6,000rpm
Gears: four-speed manual; optional two- or three-speed automatic
Capacity: 5,359cc
Bore & Stroke: 102 × 82.6mm
Maximum Speed: 240km/h (150mph)
Chassis: ladder frame. Front suspension by wishbones, coil springs, anti-roll bar, telescopic dampers. Rear suspension, live axle, semi-elliptic springs

172

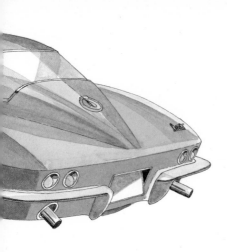

Dimensions: wheelbase 249cm (98in). Track (front) 143cm (56in); track (rear) 145cm (57in)
Brakes: four-wheel drums
Body: fastback coupé
The Stingray was a complete change from earlier Corvette models. It had a new chassis and new body, and its long, slanted nose, sporty rear deck made the car an instant hit with Corvette enthusiasts.

FORD Mustang GT

Country of Origin: USA
Date: 1964
Engine: four stroke, four cylinders in line; ohv; one downdraught twin barrel carburettor; 86hp at 4,600rpm
Gears: four-speed, fully synchronised
Capacity: 2,300cc
Bore & Stroke: 95.9 × 79.5mm
Maximum Speed: 154km/h (96mph)
Chassis: platform with front subframe. Independent front suspension by McPherson, wishbones (lower control arms), coil springs, telescopic dampers, anti-roll bar. Rear suspension rigid axle, lower trailing radius arms, upper oblique torque arms, transverse linkage bar, coil springs, telescopic dampers

Dimensions: wheelbase 255cm (100.4in). Track (front) 144cm (56.6in); track (rear) 145cm (57in)
Steering: rack-and-pinion
Brakes: front/disc; rear/drum
The Mustang won the Industrial Designers' Institute Award and, a unique event for a car, the Tiffany Gold Medal Award. In the Spring of 1964 there was media saturation of the Mustang and thousands of people flocked to the salerooms to buy this unusual new car. Within six weeks of its appearance the Mustang had become the top-selling compact car, and was seventh in the US car sales. One of its most attractive aspects was the large number of options available.

LOTUS Elan

Country of Origin: Great Britain
Date: 1964
Engine: Lotus-Ford straight four; twin ohcs; twin Weber carburettors; 105bhp at 5,500rpm
Gears: four-speed manual
Capacity: 1,558cc
Bore & Stroke: 82.55 × 72.75mm
Chassis: steel backbone; unstressed glass fibre body. Independent front suspension by wishbones, coil springs and dampers. Independent rear suspension by wishbones, coil springs and dampers
Dimensions: wheelbase 214cm (84in). Track (front) 117cm (46in); track (rear) 122cm (48in)

Brakes: four-wheel disc
The backbone chassis was a new feature of the Elan. It was made of steel, forked at either end to the suspension mountings. The transmission ran along the backbone, while the engine and gearbox were located between the prongs of the front fork. This arrangement rendered the conventional tubular chassis unnecessary. It had an integral bumper and rectractable headlights, these also being an unusual feature for the time.

PORSCHE 911

Country of Origin: Germany
Date: 1964
Engine: horizontally opposed 2-litre six-cylinder; single ohc each side; two triple-choke Solex carburettors; 130bhp at 6,100rpm
Gears: four- or five-speed, fully synchronised
Capacity: 1,991cc
Bore & Stroke: 80 × 66mm
Maximum Speed: 210km/h (130mph)
Chassis: all-steel unitary. Front suspension comprising lower wishbones, torsion bars, vertical shock absorber struts

Dimensions: wheelbase 221cm (87in). Track (front) 133.7cm (52.6in); track (rear) 132cm (52in)
Tyres: 165HR × 15
Steering: ZF rack-and-pinion
Brakes: four-wheel disc
Body: coupé

The 911 and its many derivatives and variants has been one of the staple cars in the Porsche range for over 15 years. Its appearance and styling were both elegant and aerodynamically efficient. Although capable of 210km/h (130mph), the earliest version was noisy above 160km/h (100mph). Subsequent variations such as the Targa (1965) and, outstandingly, the Turbo (1974) have maintained the 911's reputation as one of Porsche's 'supercars'.

LAMBORGHINI Miura 400GT

Country of Origin: Italy
Date: 1966
Engine: 60-degree V-12; twin ohcs per bank; six twin-choke Weber carburettors; 350bhp at 7,000rpm
Gears: five-speed manual
Capacity: 3,929cc
Bore & Stroke: 82 × 62mm
Maximum Speed: 290km/h (180mph)
Chassis: pressed steel. Independent suspension both front and rear by wishbones, coil springs, dampers, anti-roll bars
Dimensions: wheelbase 250cm (98.5in). Track 142cm (56in)
Brakes: four-wheel disc

Ferruccio Lamborghini started out as a tractor manufacturer, building his first cars as a hobby. Seeing an
opening for large, exclusive sports cars, he established a factory at Bologna. 'Miura' is the name of a
Spanish breed of bull, famous for its ferocity. The
Miura of 1966 had a new rear transverse engine;
developments eventually produced the 385bhp
Miura P400SV. It was an extremely reliable model,
and was the world's fastest production car for some
time. In the 1970s, the Countach took over this title.

FERRARI Daytona

Country of Origin: Italy
Date: 1968
Engine: 60-degree, 4.4-litre twin-cam V-12; twin ohcs per bank; six twin-choke carburettors (Weber); 352bhp at 7,500rpm
Gears: five-speed manual transaxle. Rear-mounted
Capacity: 4,390cc
Bore & Stroke: 81 × 71mm
Maximum Speed: 290km/h (180mph)
Chassis: tubular. Independent front and rear suspension comprising wishbones, coil springs, dampers and anti-roll bars

Dimensions: wheelbase 241cm (95in). Track (front) 143cm (56.5in) track (rear) 145cm (57in)
Brakes: four-wheel ventilated disc
This was one of the fastest road cars ever and was the ultimate front-engined Ferrari. The engine was placed well to the front and its rear-mounted gearbox combined with differential. The body was styled by Pininfarina, and visibility from the cockpit was good. Independent teams of drivers raced at Le Mans with good results, including a fifth in 1971, fifth, sixth, seventh, eighth and ninth in 1972. A GTO came second in the Daytona 24-Hours in 1973 and 1979.

183

DATSUN 240Z

Country of Origin: Japan
Date: 1969
Engine: straight six; single ohc; twin Hitachi (SU) carburettors; 157bhp at 5,600rpm
Gears: five-speed manual, with synchromesh
Capacity: 2,393cc
Bore & Stroke: 83 × 73.7mm
Maximum Speed: 200km/h (125mph)
Chassis: unitary. Independent suspension both front and rear, with wishbones and McPherson struts
Dimensions: wheelbase 230cm (90.5in). Track (front) 136cm (53.5); track (rear) 135cm (53in)

Brakes: front/disc; rear/drum
Body: fastback, two-seater coupé
The 240Z began where the Healey 3000 left off in
1968. Datsun studied the earlier model in detail and
developed the 2.4-litre, six-cylinder unit which was
housed in a beautifully streamlined coupé bodyshell.
It was fast, had good handling qualities and was both
economical and reliable. It won the East African
Safari Rally twice.

FERRARI Dino 246GT

Country of Origin: Italy
Date: 1969
Engine: 65-degree V-6; twin ohcs per bank; three Weber carburettors; 195bhp at 7,600rpm
Gears: five-speed manual
Capacity: 2,418cc
Bore & Stroke: 92.5 × 60mm
Chassis: steel tubular and sheet. Independent front and rear suspension by wishbones, coil springs, dampers and anti-roll bars

Dimensions: wheelbase 234cm (92in). Track (front) 142cm (56in); track (rear) 140cm (55in)
Brakes: four-wheel ventilated disc
This was the cheapest Ferrari ever marketed, but this did not imply that it was anything but an excellent car; its mechanics, performance and appearance were all superb. Despite its good performance characteristics it was never developed as a competition model and was discontinued in 1973, being replaced by the 308GT.

MARCOS 3-litre

Country of Origin: Great Britain
Date: 1969
Engine: Ford, 60-degree V-6; pushrod ohv; Weber carburettor; 136bhp at 4,750rpm
Gears: four-speed manual with overdrive
Capacity: 2,994cc
Bore & Stroke: 93.7 × 72.4mm
Maximum Speed: 200km/h (125mph)
Chassis: wooden with steel frames. Independent front suspension by wishbones, coil springs, dampers and anti-roll bar. Rear suspension by live axle, upper and lower links, Panhard rod, coil spring and dampers

Dimensions: wheelbase 227cm (89.5in). Track (front) 123cm (48.5); track (rear) 130cm (51in)
Brakes: front/disc; rear/drum

The Marcos company was formed by Jean March and Frank Costin in 1962. Costin, who had designed bodies for Lister, Lotus and Vanwall, was convinced that modern marine plywoods could be used to good effect in car construction. So, departing radically from accepted practice, the first Marcos had a wooden chassis. Its performance proved Costin right and it became popular in club racing. The use of the 3-litre Ford V-6 with its extra weight gave improved roadholding. In 1970 the wooden chassis was finally replaced with conventional steel tubes.

MORGAN Plus Eight

Country of Origin: Great Britain
Date: 1969
Engine: Rover 90-degree V-8; pushrod ohv; twin SU carburettors; 184bhp at 5,200rpm
Gears: separate four-speed manual
Capacity: 3,528cc
Bore & Stroke: 89 × 71mm
Maximum Speed: 200km/h (125mph)
Chassis: Z-section side members. Independent front suspension by vertical sliding pillars, coil springs and dampers. Rear suspension by rigid axle, semi-elliptic leaf springs and dampers

Dimensions: wheelbase 249cm (98in). Track 127cm (50in)
Brakes: front/disc; rear/drum

The Plus Eight was the most exciting Morgan of them all, causing a great stir at its appearance at the 1968 Earls Court Show. The powerful Rover $3\frac{1}{2}$-litre engine gave it phenomenal acceleration and effortless speed. Although stylistically old-fashioned, with somewhat rough suspension and barely weather-proof, the Plus Eight remains popular to this day, maintaining the Morgan tradition of open-air motoring.

JAGUAR E-Type (Series 3)

Country of Origin: Great Britain
Date: 1971
Engine: 60-degree V-12; single ohc per bank; four Stromberg carburettors; 272bhp at 5,850rpm
Gears: four-speed manual
Capacity: 5,343cc
Bore & Stroke: 90 × 70mm
Maximum Speed: 233km/h (145mph)
Chassis: monocoque. Independent front suspension by wishbones, torsion bars, dampers and anti-roll

bar. Independent rear suspension by wishbones, radius arms, coil springs and dampers
Dimensions: wheelbase 267cm (105in). Track (front) 138cm (54.25in); track (rear) 135cm (53in)
Brakes: four-wheel disc
The most famous of the Jaguar series, the E-type caused a sensation on its first appearance in 1961, having extraordinary style and performance at a very reasonable price. The Series 3 Jaguar had the long-awaited V-12 engine, a smooth and powerful unit with improved torque, and used the long wheelbase bodyshell as standard. Of the total E-type production (75,584 cars) 15,292 were V-12s. It was the last model in one of the most successful lines Jaguar produced.

LANCIA Fulvia

Country of Origin: Italy
Date: 1971
Engine: 13-degree V-4; single ohc; twin Solex carburettors; 114bhp at 6,000rpm
Gears: five-speed manual
Capacity: 1,584cc
Bore & Stroke: 82 × 75mm
Chassis: unitary with steel body. Independent front suspension by wishbones, transverse leaf spring, dampers and anti-roll bars. Rear suspension by dead axle, semi-elliptic leaf springs, dampers, Panhard rod and anti-roll bar

Dimensions: wheelbase 233cm (91.5in). Track (front) 130cm (51in); track (rear) 128cm (50.5in)
Brakes: four-wheel disc

The Fulvia was produced to replace the old Appia saloon and went through a series of developments to produce a series of successful rally cars. By the time the 1971 model appeared, the competition and road versions were not very different. Handling was good and the brakes powerful.

CHEVROLET Camaro Z-28

Country of Origin: USA
Date: 1972
Engine: 90-degree V-8; pushrod ohv; Rochester carburettors; 300bhp at 4,800rpm
Gears: four-speed manual
Capacity: 5,735cc
Bore & Stroke: 101.6 × 88.4mm
Maximum Speed: 185km/h (115mph)
Chassis: unitary. Independent front suspension by wishbones and coil springs. Rear suspension by live axle, semi-elliptic springs and optional anti-roll bar; hydraulic dampers

Dimensions: wheelbase 274cm (108in). Track (front) 155cm (61in); track (rear) 152cm (60in)
Brakes: front/disc; rear/drum
The Camaro was Chevrolet's answer to the Ford Mustang, and the high-performance Z-28 was every bit the match of the hottest of the Ford ponycars. The Camaro Z-28 remained one of the fastest American cars until the late 1970s, despite the fact that sound and emission legislation had deprived it of much of its original all-American zest.

VOLVO P1800E

Country of Origin: Sweden
Date: 1972
Engine: straight four; pushrod ohv; Bosch fuel injection; 130bhp at 6,000rpm
Gears: four-speed manual, plus overdrive
Capacity: 1,986cc
Bore & Stroke: 88.9 × 80mm
Maximum Speed: 160km/h (100mph)
Chassis: unitary. Independent front suspension comprising wishbones, coil springs, dampers, anti-roll bar. Rear suspension comprising live axle, trailing arms, Panhard rod, coil springs, dampers

Dimensions: wheelbase 239cm (94in). Track 133cm (52.5in)
Brakes: four-wheel disc
This model was the best-known sporting Volvo which, despite its rather outmoded styling and uninspiring performance, survived in the sports-car arena for over ten years, its solid reliability offsetting these other drawbacks.

LAMBORGHINI Countach

Country of Origin: Italy
Date: 1973
Engine: 60-degree 4-litre V-12; twin ohcs per bank;
six Weber 4DCOE 104-105 twin-choke carburettors;
375bhp at 8,000rpm
Gears: five-speed manual, fully synchronised
Capacity: 3,929cc
Bore & Stroke: 82 × 62mm
Maximum Speed: 280km/h (175mph)
Chassis: multi-tubular. Independent front and rear
suspension comprising wishbones, coil springs,
dampers, anti-roll bars

Dimensions: wheelbase 252cm (99in). Track (front) 150cm (59in); track (rear) 152cm (60in)
Steering: rack-and-pinion
Brakes: four-wheel disc
Body: coupé

The Countach was Lamborghini's successor to the Miura. It kept to its maker's reputation for good handling and roadholding ability. It was an expensive car to develop, and by the time it reached production the economic climate was unfavourable to such high performance cars; however Countachs were still being produced in small numbers as Lamborghini went into receivership at the end of the 1970s.

MATRA-SIMCA Bagheera

Country of Origin: France
Date: 1973
Engine: Simca straight four; pushrod ohv; twin Weber carburettors; 84bhp at 6,000rpm
Gears: Simca four-speed manual
Capacity: 1,294cc
Bore & Stroke: 76.7 × 70mm
Maximum Speed: 185km/h (115mph)
Chassis: tubular and boxed members. Independent front suspension comprising wishbones, torsion bars, dampers. Independent rear suspension comprising trailing arms, torsion bars, dampers

Dimensions: wheelbase 237cm (93.5in). Track (front) 138cm (54.5in); track (rear) 143cm (56.5in) With its aerodynamically efficient body and three-abreast seating, the Bagheera sold well from the beginning. It utilised mass-production components which kept the price at a reasonable level. The engine was situated transversely at the rear and although acceleration was not brilliant the 185km/h (115mph) top speed claimed for the Bagheera was enough to satisfy thousands of customers.

LANCIA Stratos

Country of Origin: Italy
Date: 1974
Engine: 65-degree V-6; twin ohcs per bank; three Weber carburettors; 190bhp at 7,000rpm
Gears: five-speed manual
Capacity: 2,418cc
Bore & Stroke: 92.5 × 60mm
Chassis: monocoque tubular subframes front and rear. Independent front and rear suspension comprising wishbones, coil springs, dampers, anti-roll bars.
Dimensions: wheelbase 218cm (86in). Track (front) 143cm (56.5in); track (rear) 146cm (57.5in)
Brakes: four-wheel disc

The Stratos underwent a long development pro-
gramme, being run in many Italian events between
1970 and 1974. It was homologated in 1974 and
some were used for racing, others as road cars.
While it had little success in racing, in rallying it was
extremely successful, including four Monte Carlo
Rally wins.

MASERATI Merak SS

Country of Origin: Italy
Date: 1974
Engine: 90-degree V-6; twin ohcs per bank; three twin-choke Weber carburettors; 190bhp at 6,000rpm
Gears: five-speed ZF manual
Capacity: 2,965cc
Bore & Stroke: 91.6 × 75mm
Maximum Speed: 225km/h (140mph)
Chassis: integral. Independent front and rear suspension by wishbones, coil springs, anti-roll bars, dampers
Dimensions: wheelbase 260cm (102.5in). Track (front) 147cm (58in); track (rear) 145cm (57in)
Brakes: four-wheel disc

The Merak SS was an attempt to provide a mid-engined car with sporty attributes but which also had good standards of comfort and was economical on fuel. Designed by Giugiaro, the Merak first appeared in 1972. The suspension on this earlier model gave a relatively rough ride, but this was improved on the SS model. The SS's V-6 engine was also used in the Citroen SM, and the Merak also used other Citroen components.

TRIUMPH TR7

Country of Origin: Great Britain
Date: 1975
Engine: straight four, single ohc; SU carburettors; 105bhp at 5,500rpm
Gears: four-speed manual
Capacity: 1,998cc
Bore & Stroke: 90.3 × 78mm
Maximum Speed: 174km/h (108mph)
Chassis: unitary steel monocoque. Independent front suspension comprising McPherson struts, coil springs, lower lateral links, anti-roll bar. Rear suspension comprising live axle, lower trailing arms, upper arms, coil springs, dampers, anti-roll bar
Dimensions: wheelbase 216cm (85in). Track (front) 141cm (55.5in); track (rear) 140cm (55in)

Brakes: front/disc; rear/drum, dual hydraulic circuits, vacuum servo assistance

Body: two-seater, two-door, coupé

This model was designed for the American market, which explains the exaggerated, wedge-shaped profile. The wheelbase was slightly too short and although the car had good handling qualities and was generally easily controllable, it rode rather roughly under bumpy conditions. Its racing appearance was belied by its actual performance and maximum speed, but even so it has been quite successful in both Europe and the USA. It was eventually updated as the TR8 by the addition of a five-speed gearbox and the Rover 3500 V-8 engine which gave it the power of which it looked capable.

FERRARI 512BB Berlinetta Boxer

Country of Origin: Italy
Date: 1976
Engine: flat-12 5-litre; twin ohcs per bank; four triple-choke carburettors (Weber); 340bhp at 6,800rpm
Gears: five-speed manual transaxle
Capacity: 4,924cc
Bore & Stroke: 82 × 78mm
Chassis: tubular, monocoque centre section. Independent suspension both front and rear comprising wishbones, coil springs, dampers and anti-roll bars
Dimensions: wheelbase 250cm (98.5in). Track

(front) 150cm (59in); track (rear) 151cm (59.5in)
Brakes: four-wheel ventilated disc
Body: Pininfarina-styled

The Berlinetta Boxer was considered by some to be *the* supercar of the 1970s. It was the first mid-engined Ferrari for road use, and certainly had strong claims to the supercar title. It had wider wheels than earlier BB models plus a nose-spoiler, and many customers saw it as having competition potential. However it had little success in racing apart from coming twelfth at Le Mans in 1979 and tenth in 1980.

PORSCHE 928

Country of Origin: Germany
Date: 1977
Engine: 90-degree light alloy V-8; one ohc per bank; Bosch K-Jetronic fuel injection; 240bhp at 5,850rpm
Gears: five-speed, synchronised; optional three-speed automatic
Capacity: 4,474cc
Bore & Stroke: 95 × 78.9mm
Maximum Speed: 233km/h (145mph)
Chassis: independent front suspension comprising upper and lower wishbones with coil springs, anti-roll bars. Independent rear suspension Weissach axle with coil springs and anti-roll bars

Dimensions: wheelbase 250cm (98.4in). Track (front) 154.5cm (61in); track (rear) 151cm (59.6in)
Brakes: disc. Dual circuit hydraulics, servo assistance

The luxurious, high-performance 928 won the Car of the Year Award for 1978. Although some purists considered it a less attractive-looking model than other Porsche models with its rounded tail and alloy wheels, its performance and fuel-consumption more than made up for these minor shortcomings of styling; it was a very stable car to drive.

FIAT X1/9 1500

Country of Origin: Italy
Date: 1978
Engine: straight four; single ohc; one Weber carburettor; 85bhp at 6,000rpm
Gears: five-speed manual
Capacity: 1,498cc
Bore & Stroke: 86.4 × 63.9mm
Maximum Speed: 177km/h (110mph)
Chassis: platform. Independent front suspension comprising McPherson struts and lower wishbones. Rear suspension by McPherson struts, wishbones and single links
Dimensions: wheelbase 220cm (86.5in). Track 135cm (53in)

Brakes: four-wheel disc, without servo
Body: Bertone-designed and built. Targa-type detachable roof panel

The X1/9 with its Targa top first appeared on the Targa Florio circuit in Sicily. Fiat developed this new, neat, sporty package by taking the engine from the existing Fiat 128 and inserting it in a striking, wedge-shaped body. This exciting little car can go from 0–97km/h (0–60mph) in about 12.6 seconds, and covers the standing-start kilometre in 34.5 seconds. The X1/9 is easy to control and agile, with good brakes. It is one of the latest in the tradition of sports cars which are fun to drive.

PORSCHE 911 Turbo

Country of Origin: Germany
Date: 1978
Engine: flat six; one ohc per bank; six Solex carburettors; Bosch fuel injection and turbocharger; 300bhp at 5,500rpm
Gears: four-speed manual
Capacity: 3,299cc
Bore & Stroke: 97 × 74.4mm
Maximum Speed: 260km/h (160mph)
Chassis: integral steel. Independent front suspension by McPherson struts, transverse wishbones, torsion bars and anti-roll bar. Independent rear suspension

by trailing arms, transverse torsion bars, dampers and anti-roll bar

Dimensions: wheelbase 227cm (89.5in). Track (front) 137cm (54in); track (rear) 135cm (53in)

Brakes: four-wheel disc

A direct descendent of the 1964 911 and a magnificent model from the 911 range, the Turbo caused a sensation when it first appeared at the Paris Motor Show in 1974. Its handling, cornering, braking and acceleration were all excellent. There were changes of style which distinguished it from other 911s such as a modified nose spoiler, different wheels and extended wheel arches.

PONTIAC Firebird Trans Am

Country of Origin: USA
Date: 1979
Engine: 90-degree 4.9-litre V-8; Rochester carburettor; Garrett AiResearch turbocharger; 205bhp at 4,000rpm
Gears: three-speed automatic
Capacity: 4,940cc
Bore & Stroke: 101.6 × 76.2mm
Maximum Speed: 170km/h (110mph)
Chassis: unitary. Independent front suspension comprising wishbones, lower trailing links, coil springs, dampers, anti-roll bar. Rear suspension comprising rigid axle semi-elliptic leaf springs, dampers, anti-roll bar
Dimensions: wheelbase 274cm (108in). Track (front) 155cm (61in); track (rear) 152cm (60in)
Brakes: four-wheel ventilated discs

By the late 1970s the engines of the Firebirds had to be altered to conform to stringent USA emission regulations. Several engines were available, including the 305 Chevy, 350 Chevy, 301 V-8 in two- and four-barrel versions and the 403 Oldsmobile. The 1979 model had several new features such as spoilers made in a more flexible and durable material and a wider range of colours. Out of 211,454 Firebirds produced in 1979, 117,108 were Trans Am models.

DE LOREAN Sports Car

Country of Origin: Great Britain
Date: 1980
Engine: PVR, four-stroke, six-cylinder; in line ohvs; two ohcs; 130hp at 5,500rpm
Gears: five-speed, fully synchronised
Capacity: 2,850cc
Bore & Stroke: 91 × 73mm
Maximum Speed: 209km/h (130mph)
Chassis: independent front suspension by parallel, unequal length upper and lower control arms, coil springs, coaxial telescopic dampers. Independent rear suspension by trailing arms with upper and lower unequal length parallel transverse control arms, coil springs, coaxial telescopic dampers.

Dimensions: wheelbase 241cm (95in). Track (front) 166cm (65.4in); track (rear) 159cm (62.7in)
Steering: rack-and-pinion
Brakes: disc, servo
Body: coupé, two doors
De Lorean set out to create a car which would break new ground in automotive technology; it would combine the latest safety features with good performance and fuel economy. One of the world's top stylists, Giorgetto Giugiaro, designed the car, and one of its most extraordinary features was its stainless steel external panels.

221

ASTON MARTIN Vantage

Country of Origin: Great Britain
Date: 1981
Engine: V-8; two ohcs per bank; four Weber 48 IDF/3 carburettors
Gears: five-speed manual
Capacity: 5,340cc
Bore & Stroke: 100 × 85mm
Maximum Speed: 270km/h (168mph)
Chassis: tubular steel. Independent front suspension by unequal length wishbones, co-axial coil springs and telescopic dampers, anti-roll bar. Rear suspen-

sion by de Dion axle located by parallel trailing arms and transverse Watts linkage, coil springs, telescopic dampers

Steering: rack-and-pinion

Brakes: ventilated disc

In an enthusiastic review in 1981 *Motor* magazine describes the Vantage as 'one of the finest means of travel yet devised'. *Motor* also judged it to be one of the fastest cars available at any price, capable of 0–97km/h (0–60mph) in an effortless 5.2 seconds and 100mph in 11.9 seconds.

PORSCHE 924 Carrera GTS

Country of Origin: Germany
Date: 1981
Engine: Audi four-stroke, four-cylinder, turbo-charged; ohv; single ohc; 245bhp
Gears: five-speed, fully synchronised
Capacity: 1,984cc
Bore & Stroke: 86.5 × 84.4mm
Maximum Speed: 225km/h (140mph)
Chassis: integral. Independent front suspension by McPherson, lower wishbones, coil springs, telescopic dampers, anti-roll bar. Independent rear suspension by semi-trailing arms, transverse torsion bars, coil springs, telescopic dampers, anti-roll bar

Dimensions: wheelbase 240cm (94.5in). Track (front) 147cm (58in); track (rear) 148cm (58.3in)
Tyres: front 205/55VR × 16; rear 225/50VR × 16
Steering: rack-and-pinion
Brakes: disc
Body: coupé, plastic

The first 924 Carrera appeared at the Frankfurt Motor Show in 1979. The production model came out in 1980 as the Carrera GT, this was raced at Le Mans and came sixth in the GT category. The GTS followed in 1981 with the Carrera's much-extended wheel arches and spoilers front and rear. It could be developed into a full-blown rally or racing car as the Carrera GTR.

HE 944

Country of Origin: Germany
Date: 1981
Engine: four stroke, four cylinders in line; ohv; single ohc; Bosch K-Jetronic electronic fuel injection; 165bhp at 5,800rpm
Gears: five-speed, fully synchronised, optional three-speed
Capacity: 2,479cc
Bore & Stroke: 100 × 78.9mm
Maximum Speed: 233km/h (145mph)
Chassis: integral. Independent front suspension comprising coil springs, telescopic dampers, wishbones, anti-roll bar. Independent rear suspension, Weissach

axle, wishbones, semi-trailing arms, transverse torsion bars, coil springs, telescopic dampers
Dimensions: wheelbase 240cm (94.5in). Track (front) 148cm (58.3in); track (rear) 145cm (57in)
Tyres: 185/70VR × 15
Steering: rack-and-pinion
Brakes: disc
The body design, a product of years of Porsche research and development, gives good roadholding at high speeds. It has excellent handling characteristics and is economical on fuel. It is capable of 0–97km/h (0-60mph) in 8.4 seconds. The 1986 Turbo version has reduced this to 6.3 seconds.

ALPINE RENAULT A310 V6

Country of Origin: France
Date: 1982
Engine: PRV V-6; 150bhp at 6,000rpm. One Solex 34 TBIA downdraught single barrel carburettor and one Solex 35 CEEI downdraught twin barrel carburettor; vee-slanted ohvs
Gears: five-speed fully synchronised
Capacity: 2,664cc
Bore & Stroke: 88 ×73mm
Maximum Speed: 220km/h (137mph)
Chassis: integral, central steel backbone. Independent suspension comprising wishbones, rubber elements, coil springs, anti-roll bar, telescopic

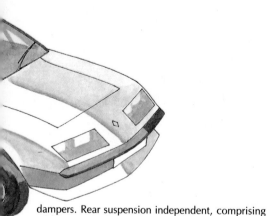

dampers. Rear suspension independent, comprising wishbones, coil springs, anti-roll bar, telescopic dampers

Tyres: 190/55VR × 13 front; 220/55VR × 14 rear

Steering: rack-and-pinion

Brakes: disc

Body: coupé, in plastic material. Two doors. 2+2 seats

This car has been in production since 1971, originally with 1.6-litre engine. The PVR V-6 engine was introduced in 1981. An earlier version won the Rallye du Var in 1976.

MERCEDES-BENZ 500SL

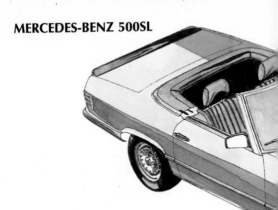

Country of Origin: Germany
Date: 1982
Engine: four-stroke, six cylinders in line; ohvs; two ohcs; Bosch K-Jetronic fuel injection; 185hp at 5,800rpm
Gears: five-speed, synchronised
Capacity: 2,746cc
Bore & Stroke: 86 × 78.8mm
Maximum Speed: 200km/h (124mph)
Chassis: integral. Independent front suspension by upper wishbones with single transverse rod, longitudinal leading arm in unit with anti-roll bar, coil springs, telescopic dampers. Independent rear suspension by oblique semi-trailing arms, coil springs,

auxiliary rubber springs, anti-roll bar, telescopic dampers
Dimensions: wheelbase 246cm (97in). Track (front) 145cm (57in); track (rear) 144cm (56.5in)
Steering: recirculating ball, damper, servo
Brakes: disc
Body: roadster, two doors.

FERRARI 308GTO

Country of Origin: Italy
Date: 1983
Engine: Ferrari 90-degree, V-8; four valves per cylinder overhead; four ohcs; Weber-Marelli electronic injection and ignition; 400hp at 7,000rpm; supercharged by two turbo-compressors
Gears: five-speed, synchronised
Bore & Stroke: 80 × 71mm
Maximum Speed: 305km/h (189.5mph)
Chassis: tubular steel. Independent front and rear suspension with Koni hydraulic shock absorbers with co-axial springs and stabiliser bars

Dimensions: wheelbase 245cm (96.5in). Track (front) 156cm (61.4in); track (rear) 156cm (61.5in)
Tyres: radial; 225/55 front, 265/50VR 16 rear
Steering: rack-and-pinion
Brakes: ventilated disc
Body: two seater Berlinetta
With its sleek, stylish bodywork designed by Pininfarina and excellent performance, the GTO shows itself to be rooted firmly in time-honoured Ferrari traditions. It is capable of 0–97km/h (0–60mph) plus in 4.9 seconds and can do the standing quarter mile in 12.7 seconds.

LAMBORGHINI Jalpa 3500

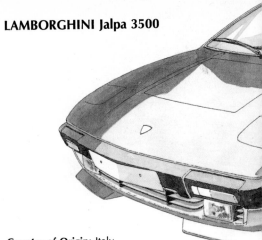

Country of Origin: Italy
Date: 1984
Engine: V-8; two ohvs per cylinder; two ohcs; four Weber 42 DCNF carburettors; 255hp at 7,000rpm
Gears: five-speed, with synchromesh on reverse gear
Capacity: 3,485cc
Bore & Stroke: 86 × 75mm
Maximum Speed: 248km/h (154mph)
Chassis: deep-drawing sheet. Independent suspension front and rear
Dimensions: wheelbase 245cm (96.5in). Track (front) 150cm (59in); track (rear) 155cm (61in)

Steering: rack-type
Brakes: disc, with booster
Body: open, two doors and two seats
The Lamborghini Jalpa is another in the long line of sleek, high performance cars. With its powerful, rear-mounted engine and sleek, aerodynamically efficient design, it is a worthy follower of its equally elegant and desirable stable mates, the Miura and the Countach.

Index

237